Identity

LIVING YOUR LIFE WITH
INFLUENTIAL PURPOSE

Blake Gideon

MASTER DESIGN PUBLISHING
FULTON, KY

Identity/Blake Gideon. – 2nd ed.
ISBN 978-1-941512-22-7

Master Design Publishing
789 State Route 94 E
Fulton, KY 42041
www.masterdesign.org

Blake Gideon personally wants to thank Josh Kidwell for his initial edits, his advice and encouragement to write this book.

Layout and Cover Design by Faithe Thomas

Printed in the USA

Contents

Preface vii

Introduction xi

Chapter 1. Identity: A View from Above 1

Chapter 2. Redeemed for His Glory 21

Chapter 3. The Truth About You 31

Chapter 4. Are You Doing Your Part? 51

Chapter 5. The Right Way to Live 71

Chapter 6. Gearing up for Battle 93

Contact Information 115

I dedicate this book to my wife and kids.
Being a husband and dad are two of my greatest joys.

I also dedicate this book to the wonderful people at
First Baptist Edmond. You make pastoring a pleasure.

Preface

Books do not just occur. They are a creative endeavor. A person exercises the will to put one word after another onto a page to make something that was not there before; at least, that is what some have said. The Bible says there is nothing new under the sun. As such, this book is no better or worse than any of the other Christian books that are available.

This one is just personal.

It contains personal testimonies of real life people whose lives have been transformed by the gospel. This is a book about the gospel. This is a book about people. This is a book about change. As a matter of fact, as you read this little book, you will also encounter my own personal story of transformation.

As with any great journey, the life of a Christian begins with the first step. In this case, the old Chinese proverb rings true, "The journey of a thousand miles begins with the first step." I believe the first step for any Christian is to know who they are in Christ. If this first step is missed or perhaps later forgotten, it can lead to a life of continual frustration, disappointment, and even depression. Many Christians have started this journey well, only to lose focus along the way. No one is more influential in your life than you. Think about it, you are in a constant dialogue with yourself all day long. So, what are you saying to yourself? Here are a few examples that might ring a note with you: "I'm so overweight," "I'm so depressed," "I'm a failure," "Nobody cares about me," "No one appreciates what I do." Or it could be, "I'm a divorced mother/father," "I'm an orphan," "I'm an addict." Of course, I could go on but I think you get the idea.

So, what is the first step in the Christian journey? It is to understand your new identity. Every human on the face of the earth has an established identity, and that means you. I am not talking about your name, social security number, or even your DNA. I'm talking about the way you see yourself and the words you speak to yourself. For example, some people determine their identity through occupation. They see themselves as a janitor, lawyer, or schoolteacher. Consequently, their occupation shapes their internal dialogue. There are others who determine their identity through past events or present circumstances. In other words, their identity is situational. When things are going well in their lives, they feel wonderful, like they are on the pinnacle of the mountain. They hear the birds chirping, they see the sun rising, and feel the soft cool breeze on a hot summer day. They are happy and cordial toward everyone they meet. Do you have the picture in your mind?

But suddenly, the situation changes, and dark clouds begin to cast their eerie blanket over the beauty of the sunrise. The birds hush their singing, and quickly they fall from the pinnacle of the mountain into the miry bog of the valley. Everything about their countenance has changed. They are no longer happy but overcome with fear and sadness. Fear causes them to lash out at others with anger and suspicion. Does this sound familiar? This is a daily reality for many, including Christians. The good news is, it doesn't have to be this way. Your perpetual ride on the emotional roller coaster can stop. Your internal negative dialogue can change. And this is what this book is all about. I hope you are ready for the journey. Let's get started.

Introduction

FINDING OUR IDENTITY IN THE BIBLE

Paul, an apostle of Christ Jesus by the will of God,
To the saints who are in Ephesus, and are faithful in
Christ Jesus: Grace to you and peace from God our
Father and the Lord Jesus Christ.
Ephesians 1:1-2

It is quite surprising that there are few personal references to the Apostle Paul in the book of Ephesians. As a matter of fact, Paul has not written what you would call a personal correspondence. This is in spite of the fact that he spent more time in Ephesus than he did at any of the other places he preached on his missionary journeys. So, one may ask, "Why no personal reference?"

During Paul's second missionary journey, he left Pricilla and Aquila, who were some of his closest helpmates, in Ephesus. Paul left saying if the grace of God allowed, then he would come back. During his third missionary journey, that is exactly what he did. He left Galatia and made his way into the interior part of Ephesus. He came and visited the church and Pricilla and Aquila. He spent three years in Ephesus preaching, eventually being forced to leave because of his powerful preaching.

The simple answer is that Ephesians is a circular letter. It was not meant just for the church at Ephesus, it was meant for all churches. Paul wrote the letter, and the letter was copied but the name of the church was left blank. If the letter was going to Ephesus, they would fill in the name of the church at Ephesus or Philippi. It was not meant for just one church but for all the churches. By extension, then, it was meant for all churches throughout all time. It was meant for us too.

If we read it as though it were meant for us as well, we can look at verse one and think, "Paul an apostle...to the faithful saints at [Your Church]." He says, "Grace to you and peace from God our Father and the Lord Jesus Christ." In verse 3, he identifies the source of our blessing, "Praise God..." Let us never forget that we are who we are by God's grace. It is not something we earn or deserve. It is by God's grace. So Paul says, "Praise God the Father of our Lord Jesus Christ." Why are we to give Him all the glory? "He has blessed us in Christ with every spiritual blessing."

Because of that, my prayer is that this message would sink deep within our hearts as believers and as readers of this book and that each of us would have the determination to claim our biblical identity. I pray that we would receive it as the word of God and not as the word of man. That each of us would resolve every single day to live our lives in light of our biblical identity.

Maybe you are thinking, I have beat myself up and I have allowed others to beat me up. For too long, I have identified myself by something that has happened to me in the past. Divorced, cancer patient, abortion, bankruptcy, orphaned, or a failure. Maybe that is how you have seen yourself and thought about yourself. Does this type of thinking shape your internal dialogue? If you are a Christian, that is not your identity. Perhaps you have had a moral failure. That is not your identity. If you have repented and trusted in Christ, that is not who you are, not anymore. As you read on through this book, you will discover that in the eyes of God, "You are blessed. You are chosen. Adopted." This is by no means an excuse to sin more. The grace of God demands that we turn from sin. After all, Jesus died on the cross in order to set us free from the cruel taskmaster of sin.

Perhaps your life is falling apart and you are unable to love, or you find it hard to love. If you were honest, your life is characterized by darkness and not light. Maybe you even feel justified in your hate or anger because someone has hurt you. When you allow yourself to abide in darkness because of what someone else has done toward you, you only hurt yourself. Those closest to you may feel pushed away. Trust me, I know this from experience. As I did, you must choose to forgive. If you do not, you may fall into the pit of victimization. Where you always see yourself as a victim, and not a victor in Christ.

Horizontal versus Vertical Identity

You will determine your identity by one of two methods. You will either have a *vertical identity* that is determined by God, prayer, and His Word, or you will have a *horizontal identity* that is determined by everyone else and the world at large.

When your identity is horizontal, you are living a worldly life. Your emotions will be based upon what other people say about you. Your actions will be based on what other people think or be determined by your job. If you base your identity on anything but Jesus, your identity is a horizontal one and you are making a huge mistake.

If you are a Christian, your identity is to be determined vertically. The Spirit and the Word of God should direct all your emotions, actions, hobbies and ideas. You have a choice, dear Christian. Either you are going to look to people, circumstances, body image, or occupation to determine your identity, or you are going to choose to see yourself as Christ sees you.

At this point, I would like to share a bit of my own personal testimony. I grew up on a farm in rural Southeastern Oklahoma. I attended a small country church named Kent Baptist with my mom and sister. One Sunday morning after the pastor finished his sermon, my sister went forward to trust Christ as her personal Lord and Savior. I saw that this pleased my mother, so I followed. Within a few weeks, she and I were both baptized. However, I really did not want anything to do with Christ, even after being baptized. Later in life, I learned that there was nothing genuine about my decision.

When I was sixteen, my mother and father divorced. My father kept the farm and my mother chose to leave. I did not want my mother to be on her own, so I went with her. This decision put a strain on my relationship with my father for many years. After the divorce, my father was working all the time and I did not see him very much. My mother was working two jobs just to pay the bills. Consequently, I was a young teenage boy with very little parental supervision. Throughout high school and on into my early twenties, I lived a life of sinful rebellion. I was all about self-gratification and nothing else.

My identity was in sports, looks, and what other people thought of me. I always wanted to be known as the tough guy, the guy nobody messed with, so I got into a lot of fights. I was a very angry young man. My whole identity was wrapped up in the things of this world. I was on an emotional rollercoaster that seemed to have no end. After high school, I went to work on an offshore drilling rig in the Gulf of Mexico. Money was really good on the rig. Soon, my identity began to shift. Now I wanted to make as much money as I could. I bought a new truck and had a lot of expensive habits and hobbies. Man, I thought I was something.

It was during my time of working offshore that I came face-to-face with death. One night I was assigned the task of offloading materials from a supply boat. It was stormy this particular night. As the small boat was being violently storm-tossed, a cable hit me in the legs launching me overboard. I tried to fight against the current, but the waves were too powerful.

The pounding waves carried me further into the dark waters of the Gulf. I drifted so far that I could no longer see the lights of the rig. The crew on the boat immediately began to look for me, but they could not see me because of the high waves. Two hours went by and I had given up hope of being saved. I was lost. My heart was full of despair. I was gripped with fear. Suddenly, in the midst of the darkness, a light appeared bursting through the turbulent waves. It was a boat equipped with a searchlight. After some time of searching, they finally found me. I was saved.

It's hard to believe that it has been over twenty years since I worked on that rig. You might think that after a near-death experience like that I would turn my life over to Christ. But I was still obstinate toward the Lord and absorbed in my own fleshly impulses. After my near-death experience on the rig, I resigned my position and went to work for the Kiamichi Railroad. Once again, I was making really good money, especially for a young, single man. Along with the money came relationships. I jumped from one relationship into another like most people change shirts. Incredibly, now I added relationships to my identity. As I shopped around for significance, nothing seemed to satisfy. Fulfillment escaped me with every new worldly addition to my life.

It was during this time in my life I met a beautiful, young woman (Kelly) who is now my wife. While we were dating, I started attending church with her. After about a year we were married. Would you believe that after we were married, I immediately stopped going to church? I was a die-hard genuine hypocrite. The only reason I was going to church was to win her parents over. But as soon as we were married, I had no reason to keep going, so I thought.

Kelly was faithful to attend even if I did not go, but I could tell I was pulling her down. Late one Monday night there was a knock on our door. It was a leader from the church Kelly had visited and he wanted to meet me. At the end of our visit, he invited me to church. Reluctantly, the next Sunday I went. Soon, one Sunday turned into two, then three and so on. God really began to work on my heart. He began to show me my hypocrisy and my lust for sin. Each time I would hear the gospel, it would cut me deeply. Finally, I could not handle it any longer; I broke under the conviction of the Holy Spirit. The date was April 14, 2000, when I genuinely surrendered my life to Christ for salvation. At that moment, my identity changed forever. No longer was my identity determined in the horizontal things of this world (tough guy, liked by everybody, the life of the party, hard worker, money maker, etc.) but in a vertical relationship with Jesus Christ.

Do you see how my identity changed? Before salvation, I saw myself as a jock, somebody important, a tough guy. But on the inside, I was a very insecure young man. Because of that insecurity, my self-dialogue constantly communicated that I needed to prove myself to others. When I found their approval, I was happy, but when I did not, I would become angry, lashing out in order to intimidate. Trust me when I say, as a young man, my life was in disarray. That is until I met Christ, and then everything changed.

• CHAPTER 1 •

Identity: A View from Above

Blessed be the God and Father of our Lord Jesus Christ, who has blessed us in Christ with every spiritual blessing in the heavenly places, even as He chose us in Him before the foundation of the world, that we should be holy and blameless before Him. In love He predestined us for adoption as sons through Jesus Christ, according to the purpose of His will, to the praise of His glorious grace, with which He has blessed us in the Beloved.
Ephesians 1:3-6

Most Christians study their Bibles and read Christian books because of a desire to draw nearer to God. When a Christian reads the Word of God, they are hearing the voice of God. His Word speaks to us through the Holy Spirit and creates a desire to live life in a way that makes us an influence for the kingdom of God and advances the gospel. God wants to use your life to influence the lives of other people.

A View from Above

I want us to try to see ourselves, if we can, from God's perspective. If you are a Christian, I want you to think about a few things as we go through this together.

How does God see you and what does God say about you?

I think the answers to these questions will be of great encouragement. I pray that anyone reading this might take whatever comes. If it is a rebuke from God, then do something about it. If it is a call to repentance, then repent. If you need to be saved, then, by all means, surrender your life to Christ in repentance and faith. I pray that you will allow the Holy Spirit to do what He wants to do in your life. That is the very best thing one can do. I have told my children many times that the Christian life is based mostly on being able to admit that you are wrong and that God is right. I know from experience that God is always right. If you are convicted of sin as you read through this, let the Lord speak to you through His Word. Be submissive to Him and have a humble spirit

The Iditarod

One of the most famous sporting events in the world did not actually begin as a sporting event. Each year, mushers and their dogs race more than a thousand miles for several days from Anchorage to Nome, over some of the roughest territory in Alaska. The race is known the world over as the Iditarod. In 1925, though, it was not a famous race. There was a desperate attempt to save hundreds of children in Nome, Alaska who had been diagnosed with Diphtheria. Many of the children were dying across the country from this disease at this time and there was no vaccine. There was only a limited amount of serum that could treat it and there just happened to be about 300,000 doses of the serum in Anchorage, Alaska.

The problem was, and this is something we may have trouble getting a grip on in the 21st century, there was no real way to get from Anchorage to Nome. There was no highway. There was not even an ice road or a railroad. They could have flown the distance as powered flight had reached Alaska in the 1920s. It seems that it would have made more sense to fly than mush.

There was, however, the matter of the blizzard. Nome is very close to the Arctic Circle. The port was iced in from fall to early summer. There was no way to get the cure to Nome in any reasonable amount of time to save the children who were dying.

They would have died without the mushers.

A musher is a person with a sled and sled dogs who can travel great distances very quickly. About 150 of them were lined up along the sled trail that wound from

Anchorage to Nome. They set out and relayed the medicine from one sled to the next

In their haste to save the children, they desperately pushed onward to get the medicine to Nome. Incredibly, they made the journey in 127 hours, a record which, to this day, has never been beaten.

The Iditarod is now a famous sporting event held annually. There is a huge website about it where you can view stats and profiles for sled dogs and musher teams. Current times for each event can be viewed and record attempts are updated along with their successes and their failures. It is no longer a mission of mercy. It is a spectacle. It is entertainment.

The church could fall into the same pattern if care is not taken.

The Church

The Church was created by God to be a saving mission, and those who need it are not distant. They are our neighbors. They are our co-workers and our friends. They are the people we encounter every day. All around us, people are dying with the disease of sin, and the only cure for that disease is the gospel of the Lord Jesus Christ. That is the only medicine they need. That is the truth the world needs to hear.

We as the Church, the Body of Christ, have the only cure for the disease that is plaguing our society and our world. If we look at the Iditarod as an example, we see that when you take passion and zeal to deliver the right medicine, lives are saved. The gospel forever changes lives.

So, why are we not seeing this change more often?

Why is it that across the board, many denominations are not just plateaued, they are in decline? Why are members leaving the church never to return? Why are baptisms in decline?

It is not that the gospel has lost its power, the power of God unto salvation. The issue is with the Church. We have lost our zeal. We have lost our passion to do whatever it takes to make sure that the gospel gets from the end of our nose to the ends of the earth.

My prayer is that God would ignite revival in His churches. I pray that it would begin with me and catch fire in my church and that you would join me in that prayer. Understanding your vertical/biblical identity plays an essential role in helping the church fulfill its God-given mandate of making disciples. C.S. Lewis once said, "The church exists for nothing else but to draw men into Christ, to make them little Christs." He does not mean that we will become divine like Christ, but that we are to reflect the character of Christ in everything we do and say and to all people. You need to hear this: it is absolutely impossible to reflect the character of Christ if you are establishing your identity horizontally.

The Gospel

I hope you understand that we are obligated to share the gospel with everyone. Paul writes, "I am obligated to both the Jew and the Gentile." That is pretty much everyone from a biblical perspective. Why did he feel this way? Because although he knew he was worthy of death as a result of his sin, and was separated from God and under His wrath, he had been saved by the gospel. This is the position of anyone who has not been saved, but God, by His glorious grace, saved Paul and this changed his life. Paul's very nature was changed by the gospel. His very identity, his mission, and his purpose in life changed as a result of the gospel. Paul's new identity in Christ determined everything he did.

In Acts 8, Saul (Paul) was on his way to Damascus with letters from the high priest to have Jewish Christians there delivered into his hands for judgment. This is the same man who we see in Acts chapter 7 standing in approval holding the garments of those who were stoning Stephen to death. Yet, when he came to a saving faith in Christ, he was changed. He was no longer the greatest opponent of the Church. He became Paul the Apostle. As a result of this new peace and love, a new mission had been birthed in him. As a result of being sealed with the Holy Spirit, he was now under obligation to preach the gospel that had saved him. He was a man driven by his new identity. He did not mope around focusing on how he had persecuted the Church. Of course, he was sorry, but this was no longer his identity. He did not allow himself to be identified by his past. What about you? Are there things in your past that Christ has forgiven you of, but you keep holding onto them? Are there tragic events that Christ has given you victory over, but you keep living like a victim? If so, I pray you will follow Paul's example of leaving these things behind. Move forward in victory with your new identity in Christ.

You are who you are in Christ because of the gospel. What is the gospel? The good news that Jesus Christ is God's son who left the glories of heaven to become clothed in human flesh in order to dwell among us. Jesus Christ, Immanuel, God with us. He obeyed the law of God perfectly. He was fully man, fully God, and perfectly both. He went to the cross and died in your place. He bore the penalty of your sin, and, after absorbing the full cup of God's wrath, He died a real human death in your place. He gave up His life on the cross for you. He sacrificially surrendered His life as your sin substitute.

His lifeless body was taken from the cross by some of His disciples, prepared for burial, and placed in a borrowed tomb. It was only borrowed because three days later, He rose from the dead. That was why Paul was able to say that Christ died for our sins. He was buried and He was raised again according to the Scriptures. That is the good news, the death, burial, and resurrection of Jesus

Christ. You have sinned as has all humanity. Consequently, along with the entirety of the human race, you have all fallen short of the glory of God. The wages of sin is death but praise be to God that He demonstrated His love for us in that while we were yet sinners, Christ died for us. Therefore, if you confess with your mouth that Jesus is Lord and you believe in your heart that God has raised Him from the dead, you will be saved. That is the gospel message, and you are who you are because of it.

When we begin to understand who we are in Christ, I believe that we will burn with the zeal and passion it requires to take the gospel to our neighbor across the street, to our co-workers, to our friends, and to the people we come into contact with every day, and even to the lost in the major cities of North America and eventually to the last frontier regions of our world. The gospel should affect all of our relationships and all of our possible relationships.

It begins by understanding who you have become as a result of the gospel. The book of Ephesians will serve as our guide on this very encouraging journey. Paul wrote,

Blessed be the God and Father of our Lord Jesus Christ, who has blessed us in Christ with every spiritual blessing in the heavenly places, even as He chose us in Him before the foundation of the world, that we should be holy and blameless before Him. In love He predestined us for adoption as sons through Jesus Christ, according to the

purpose of His will, to the praise of His glorious grace,
with which He has blessed us in the Beloved.
Ephesians 1:3-6

If you are a Christian, and I hope you are, you will see in verse 3 that God has blessed you in Christ with "every spiritual blessing." Let that sink in for a moment. There is no need to get more of the Holy Spirit every Sunday. You do not need to keep going back to the well to get water. When you experienced salvation, you became "a spring of water welling up to eternal life" (John 4:14). Your life should well up with this water, and it should overflow into the lives of others who are thirsty. People who are not saved are dying of thirst for what you have: the Word of God and all that it brings. As a believer, you have all of that. Yet so often, if you're like me, you do not share it. John 4:13 says of the lost, "Everyone who drinks of this water will be thirsty again." The water Jesus is talking about here is the water of the world, which is not water at all. The pure water of the Word of God not only quenches our thirst, but also wells up in us when we are saved as a spring of living water so that we never have to drink from the sinful salt water of the world again.

Notice, He does not say He will bless you with every spiritual blessing. It says He has blessed you with every spiritual blessing. If you are a Christian, this is what the Word of God says about you. I do not know how you feel today, but if you are a believer, your life ought to be spent in praise to God for this very reason: Every spiritual blessing in the Heavens is already yours in Christ Jesus.

Ephesians 1:3-6 specifically does not say that every person in the world is blessed like this. It is directed specifically at the Christian. When Paul uses the word "us," he is talking about the Church. Us as in believers and, as we have already discussed, when he says, "To the saints who are in Ephesus," this applies to the whole Church at large in the world today. The lost/unsaved do not share in these spiritual blessings because they do not share in the Spirit of God. This is the direct result of failing to trust in Christ alone for salvation.

Also, notice that he is not talking about material blessings. I'm sure you know that you have whatever you have because of the grace of God. You have clothes on your back, a place to live, and food to eat because of God. God provides for the needs of His children. But Paul says you have "spiritual blessings." Let's take a look at a few of these spiritual blessings.

Spiritual Blessings

Love

God's love has been poured out into the heart of every person who has been born again. Thus, the spiritual blessing includes the love of God poured out into your heart. Romans 5:5 says "...hope does not put us to shame, because God's love has been poured into our hearts through the Holy Spirit who has been given to us."

God has given you the love that you need to be secure and confident in Him. He has also given you the love that you need so that you can love every other person in the same way that He loves you.

Peace

Not only has a love of God been put into your heart, He has also given you His peace. Jesus said, "Peace I leave with you; my peace I give to you. Not as the world gives do I give to you. Let not your hearts be troubled, neither let them be afraid" (John 14:27). Peace is the deep abiding security that no matter what you go through in life, you know God is in control. You have peace in knowing that true life, eternal life, awaits those who have surrendered their lives to Christ. It also includes knowing that through Christ, you are a friend of God.

Joy

Jesus also said, "These things I have spoken to you, that my joy may be in you, and that your joy may be full" (John 15:11). Joy is knowing that no matter what you go through in life, God is enough. He is all you need. This is an overwhelming sense of contentment, being satisfied with what you have in Christ. You and I both know there are a lot of losses in this world. The world loves to take away and never restore. Living this side of heaven means heartache and heartbreaks, but joy enables you to be content through it all. Joy enables you to press on and keep going when everything around seems like it is falling apart. Because you have all you need in Jesus.

Strength

Paul himself wrote, "I can do all things through Him who strengthens me" (Philippians 4:13). Notice what he wrote: Christ strengthens him. Strength is the power to stand no matter what life throws your way. The origin or the genesis of this power is not found in yourself. No matter how strong you may think you are, without Christ you are doomed to failure. On the other hand, the strength that Christ supplies is more than adequate to defeat all the powers of darkness and sin.

Fruit

This really could be the summation of all that has been written as it relates to spiritual blessings. Paul wrote, "But the fruit of the Spirit is love, joy, peace, patience, kindness, goodness, faithfulness, gentleness, self-control; against such things there is no law" (Galatians 5:22-23). I hope this is encouraging to you. All these wonderful virtues are in you as a result of God's indwelling Spirit. The Spirit indwells every believer at the moment of salvation.

In summary, you have been given everything you need to live a life of godliness. Peter wrote, "His divine power has granted to us all things that pertain to life and godliness, through the knowledge of Him who called us to His own glory and excellence" (2 Peter 1:3). In Him, you have been made complete. Paul wrote, "For in Him the whole fullness of deity dwells bodily, and you have been filled in Him, who is the head of all rule and authority" (Colossians 2:9-10).

What does it mean to be blessed with every spiritual blessing in Christ? What has the gospel done for you? You have the love, joy, peace, patience, kindness, goodness, faith, gentleness, self-control, and the strength of God. He has given you everything that you need to live your life in a way that reflects His glory. In Him, you have been made complete. He has not left you in want.

You might say, "But I do not feel complete. I do not experience peace all the time. I am a Christian. I do not experience joy all the time. I am a Christian. Why is it hard to be patient? I am a Christian. I should have the strength of God, but I feel weak. Why?"

You may not like the answer, but it is the truth according to the Word of God, so I hope you listen to it.

Galatians 5:16 says, "Walk according to the spirit and you will not carry out the desires of the flesh." If you are not experiencing these things, it is because you are not living by the Spirit. The Word of God tells us that He has given us everything that we need. We have been blessed with EVERY spiritual blessing. Start walking by the Spirit, and you will not carry out the desires of the flesh. Start living vertically, and you will no longer be concerned about the horizontal. But no matter what, God sees you as blessed.

Not only do you have every spiritual blessing, you have every spiritual blessing in the "heavenlies." What that means is, they are permanently fixed. They cannot be taken away from you. They are in the heavens. That does not mean that you have to go to heaven before you experience them. This simply means, their source is from heaven. Spiritual blessings come down to us from heaven. We will not be able to experience them in their perfection until we get there because of the flesh, but we have them now. And because they are in the heavens, they are permanent. Your joy, your peace, those things you have as a result of the gospel will always be with you. One day in heaven you will not have to fight at all to experience them because in heaven the flesh will be gone.

Until that day, walk according to the Spirit so that you will not carry out the desires of the flesh. Feed the spiritual man. Put to death the man of flesh. Take great joy in knowing that God sees you as blessed.

Even as He chose us in Him before the foundation of the world, that we should be holy and blameless before Him.
Ephesians 1:4

In verse 4, we see, "He chose us in Him before the foundation of the world." This is what is called, in theological terms, election. Some people gasp when they hear that word. Election. They also tense up when they hear the word predestination. People should not tense up. Election and predestination are both Biblical words. They are right out of the Scripture. Biblical words should not make us tense up. As a matter of fact, the word translated by the English word "chosen" in the Greek text is the word *electos*, and it is where we get the word "election." When I realized that I am who I am because God chose me and predestined me to adoption to be His son, it filled me with reverence and humility. It should not cause people to be prideful. If it does, then they have a warped theology. I did not do anything to earn my salvation. God chose me.

Is not that the proper response to God's sovereignty? Is not that the proper response to God's election? I had a theology professor who used to say, "Theology should always lead to doxology/worship." That should be your proper response to this. Not to say that you or I will have it all figured out or make ourselves think that we are smarter than someone else because WE have it narrowed down to a certain amount of points and THEY do not have any points at all. That is not the purpose. It is not for you to brag about, become puffed up, or even confused. Furthermore, the purpose is not for us to neglect evangelism. You should not say, "I do not weep over the lost because God is going to save whoever He wants to save." No. If your theology does not cause you to weep or have a burden for the lost, then your theology is from Hell and not from Heaven. Jesus Himself came for the lost, went after the lost, wept for the lost, and died for the lost. He is our Lord, but He is also our example.

The idea of God's election is throughout the Bible. God chose Abraham over all the people of his day. Not only did God choose Abraham, God also chose the nation of Israel over all the other nations. Jesus chose the twelve disciples over all the other fisherman and tax collectors. According to the *Baptist Faith and Message 2000*, "Election is the gracious purpose of God according to which He regenerates, justifies, sanctifies, and glorifies sinners. It is consistent with the free agency of man and comprehends all the means in connection with that end. It is the glorious display of God's Sovereign goodness. It is infinitely wise, holy and unchangeable. It excludes boasting and promotes humility."

John A. Broadus, one of our Baptist theologians from years gone by, once said that God's "sovereign election and man's responsibility is like looking at a house. When I stand on the front yard and look at it, I cannot see all the corners of the house. I am limited because I am a finite man. All I can see is the front of the house and maybe part of the side at one time but I cannot see all the corners at the same time. If I were going to have to see all the corners at the same time I would have get way above it and look down. When we talk about election and Man's moral responsibility all we can see are portions of it, but when God looks down from heaven, He can see the whole thing. It is a divine mystery. God is sovereign in His election. Man is also morally accountable to choose to believe." How can both be true?

Well, in the famous words of Charles Spurgeon, "God's sovereign election and man's moral responsibility are two parallel lines that run together in Scripture, two truths that run side by side." Someone once asked him, "How do you reconcile the two?" His reply was, "Friends do not need to be reconciled." You must realize that it is a divine mystery that you must embrace, but will never comprehend. Bask in the glory of God's infinite wisdom and let the mystery remain. If you are not careful you will miss the point of it all and fall into needless arguments.

In the Greek text, Ephesians 1:3-16 is one, long sentence. Paul gets so caught up in talking about the majesty and the sovereignty of the grace of God that he just explodes with exuberance and it flows out of him in one, long sentence. Paul acknowledges both sovereign election and man's responsibility here in this same sentence. In one breath, God chose you in Him before the foundation of the world, but you are morally accountable to believe the gospel. How can both be true? Do not ask me to explain it, even though I have a doctorate in this sort of thing. Theologians have been trying throughout Church history to figure it out, and honestly, it is just the second best way to start an argument in a group of preachers (the first being a discussion about eschatology or the end times), but do we have to figure it out? When we do, if we ever think we do, humility goes out the window. If we can narrow it down to a certain number of points, then pride sets up residence in its place.

Not only did God choose you, but God knew before the foundation of the world that He would send His son to die for you for the purpose of adoption. In love, He predestined us to adoption (v.5). That is why Paul was able to say, "For you have not received the spirit of slavery leading to fear but you have received the spirit of adoption where you can cry Abba, Father" (Romans 8:15). Abba is the Aramaic equivalent of "daddy." The God of heaven who spoke the world into existence and created you says that as a result of the gospel, you are adopted. He says, "You are one of My children now and you can call Me Daddy."

What a beautiful picture of the gospel in our day, when a family adopts a child, and that child is theirs. That child receives the same inheritance as their natural children. You are a joint heir with Jesus. You receive the same inheritance that Christ receives. There is one difference: when a natural family adopts a child, no matter how hard they try, that family can never change that child's DNA.

They will never be biologically related, but spiritual adoption changes you. Your spirit is changed and you take on the nature of Christ through the new birth. God says, "You are Mine. You are My precious child. I chose you and I adopted you. I have poured My love out into you."

Before moving onto the next chapter, I asked Lauren Nelson Faram (former Miss America 2007) to share her own identity story with you entitled, "Crowns and Titles."

Long before I actually wore the Miss America crown, my identity was wrapped up in that accessory. For a long time, the choices I made, the things I did and didn't do, the people I spent time with, even what I ate was all decided with that crown and title in mind.

I watched Miss America growing up and was in awe of the women who competed, but never in my wildest dreams did I ever think I could be one of them, much less, Miss America. I am so thankful God's plans are bigger than we can dream. In 2006, I was given the awesome honor of being crowned Miss Oklahoma and six short months later, I was standing on the Miss America stage hearing my name announced as Miss America 2007. That moment was probably the scariest moment of my life and the most exciting moment of my life up to that point. My life changed in an instant and I went from a small-town Oklahoma girl to representing the country as Miss America. I embarked on a year of travel doing some of the coolest things I could imagine. From meeting President George W. Bush to serving sick kids and their families through Children's Miracle Network Hospitals, I was quite literally living out my childhood dream, but even though things seemed perfect on the outside, behind closed doors it was the darkest, most lonely time of my life.

As I look back on that time in my life, I can see how I was relying on everything else but God to be my sufficiency. I was relying on an unhealthy relationship with a boyfriend to be my source of joy. I was relying on this worldly accolade called Miss America to be my identity. I relied on what people said and thought about me, good or bad, to give me my value and worth.

In March of 2007, I met Robin Marsh, a local news anchor. She was on an assignment to do a story with my mom and me for a series for Mother's Day. Little did I know that chance encounter would lead to eternal salvation for me. I went on throughout my year of service falling in love with the job of Miss America. As I placed the crown on the new Miss America's head in January of 2008, my life changed in an instant again. My time as Miss America had ended and I moved back to my hometown. I wondered what life was supposed to look like after Miss America. I felt as if I had peaked at 21 and had nowhere to go from there. I felt purposeless, lost, alone, and sad. That is when I got a call from Robin.

Robin reached out to me and invited me to grab a cup of coffee with her, and a friendship blossomed. We began getting together regularly to work out and chat, and soon she invited me to do a bible study with her in her home. She also invited me to attend church with her and her family where I met my now husband, Randy. It was through my friendship with Robin and dating relationship with Randy that I learned about a relationship with God. I saw in Robin's life how she had joy in spite of bad circumstances and had an un-

wavering faith in God's goodness. I saw in Randy's life how a relationship with Jesus had changed him and made him a man who valued my holiness and God's will above his desires. I saw that salvation was a relationship, not a to-do list and a do-not-do list. I knew they had something of supreme, eternal value and I wanted it.

It was July 4th of 2008, and I was asked to sing some patriotic songs at a concert in my hometown. I sang my songs and sat down to listen to a message from a preacher. He gave an invitation at the end and asked everyone to look to the person to his or her right or left and ask them if they wanted someone to go down with them to make a decision to follow Jesus. Randy asked me if I wanted him to go down with me, but I told him I didn't need to do that. In that moment, it was like the Lord was knocking on the door of my heart, asking if I was going to let this moment, this opportunity pass me by. I grabbed Randy's hand and went down to the front to make a decision for Jesus.

I know that was the beginning of my journey with Jesus, but it was not until October of 2011 that I truly surrendered my life to Jesus. I jumped into the deep end of church life, becoming a Sunday school teacher and worship leader, but I had never truly been transformed by a relationship with Jesus. I was still living with the shame and guilt of past mistakes, but on that Sunday in October, I surrendered my life, my shame, my guilt, and my heart to the One who knows me and loves me best.

Where I was once purposeless, I now have purpose in Jesus. I realize that the title of Miss America is a platform that opens doors to opportunities to share Jesus

> *with people. Where I was once lost and alone, I now have a Savior who is for me and with me no matter what. Where I was once sad, I now know the joy that comes from knowing I am secure and safe in the arms of Jesus. Where my identity had once been wrapped up in the crown and title of Miss America, I now know my identity is found in Jesus. I know that in Him I am blessed, chosen, adopted, saved, and sealed, and that will never change.*

Wow! I think you would agree that is a wonderful story of the grace of God. Lauren's identity went from horizontal to vertical, and everything changed. She now sees herself as blessed, chosen and adopted into the family of King Jesus.

CHAPTER 2

Redeemed for His Glory

In Him we have redemption through His blood, the forgiveness of our trespasses, according to the riches of His grace, which He lavished upon us, in all wisdom and insight making known to us the mystery of His will, according to His purpose, which He set forth in Christ as a plan for the fullness of time, to unite all things in Him, things in heaven and things on earth.

In Him we have obtained an inheritance, having been predestined according to the purpose of Him who works all things according to the counsel of His will, so that we who were the first to hope in Christ might be to the praise of His glory. In Him you also, when you heard the word of truth, the gospel of your salvation, and believed in Him, were sealed with the promised Holy Spirit, who is the guarantee of our inheritance until we acquire possession of it, to the praise of His glory.
Ephesians 1:7-14

Earlier in the book, I stated that for many years I sought my identity in the material things of this world. For example, there were times when I sought my identity in people. I was always concerned about what other people thought of me. Body image was another stronghold in my life. When I was skinny, I felt good about myself, but when I started to gain weight, I struggled with depression. Other people seek their identity in money. They feel like they need to make a certain amount of money to feel important. Maintaining a certain social status is what drives them daily. Sports are another source of identity for many. This is not just true for kids, but for many of their parents as well. Often, parents will seek to live vicariously through their children. This is often noticeable in how hard they push their children to succeed. Our society holds higher education in high regard. Sadly, many professing believers determine their identity by how many or few degrees they have hanging on their wall.

These are just a few examples. As you well know, much more could be listed. All the above are false substitutes for the believer's true identity. If you fail to determine your identity daily in Christ, you will shop around horizontally for a false substitute. Making this mistake will negatively affect your overall well-being.

To be totally transparent, after my conversion, I continued to struggle with vertical identity (and still do today). Early in ministry, my identity was pastor. That's truly how I identified myself. You may think what's wrong with that? It is wrong on every level. Let me explain. Because that was my identity, when things were going well in the church, I felt like I was the best pastor and everybody loved me. I'm sure many of you know things don't always go well in the church. Let's just say when the church would hit a sour note (more like the sound of your scream after shutting your finger in the car door); I would easily feel depressed. I felt like a horrible pastor and that everyone hated me. The roller coaster of emotion was brutal and still is when I let it be.

What has changed? Now I see myself as God's blessed, chosen, adopted child who just happens to be a husband to Kelly, a father to Seth, Matthew, Caleb and Ashlyn and the pastor of Edmond's First Baptist Church in Edmond, Oklahoma. I hope now you are beginning grasp hold of the vertical identity.

In Him we have redemption through His blood,
the forgiveness of our trespasses,
according to the riches of His grace...
Ephesians 1:7

I told you it gets better. You are redeemed (v.7). Having blessed God for His election and adoption of men and women in Christ, Paul next praises God for His redemption. Redemption is a beautiful word. It carries the idea of liberation from imprisonment and bondage. Before salvation, every person is held captive by the power of sin. However, in Christ, we are set free both from sin's power and sin's penalty, which is death (Romans 6:23). Paul's concept of redemption has its origin in the Old Testament, where redemption describes the release of a slave. Specifically, it refers to God's deliverance of His people from bondage in Egypt.

It is also important to note that our redemption in Christ was not cheap. It was made available through the blood of Christ. Peter wrote, "Knowing that you were ransomed from the futile ways inherited from your forefathers, not with perishable things such as silver or gold, but with the precious blood of Christ, like that of a lamb without blemish or spot" (1 Peter 1:18-19). The violent death of Jesus on the cross was the source of our redemption (see also 1 Corinthians 6:20).

As believers, we still struggle with sin, but we are no longer in bondage to sin. God does not see you as a sin lusting enemy anymore. He sees you as a captive that has been set free. He sees you as redeemed and He speaks of you as one who has been set free.

Not only are you redeemed, but you are also forgiven (v.7). You are not only set free from the bondage of sin, but rescued from God's judgment as well. The word "forgive" literally means, "to send away." The penalty of sin, which is death, i.e., eternal hell fire, is sent away when a sinner turns to Christ in repentance and faith (Luke 13:3;

Ephesians 2:8-9). Christ carried the burden of your sin on the cross (1 Peter 2:24). As a result of Christ's finished work (i.e. His death, burial, and resurrection), every believer in Christ is declared not guilty. Yes, this includes you (2 Corinthians 5:21).

This is the best news you have ever received. To know that you stand before God justified, declared not guilty, forgiven. Such grace is truly beyond our comprehension. Dear friend, if you are saved, when God's speaks your name, He speaks of you as forgiven. For example, when Satan accuses you before God, God responds to the enemy's allegations by declaring you as righteous. Such righteousness is yours based on the death, burial, and resurrection of Jesus Christ. This imputed righteousness can never be taken away.

Making known to us the mystery of His will, according to His purpose, which He set forth in Christ...
Ephesians 1:9

There is more! God has granted you His divine wisdom (v.9). A mystery is something that is hidden until it is to be revealed. In Christ, we are part of God's eternal purpose to gather together "all things in Christ." The dividing wall between others' ethnics has been torn down in Christ. You are now a part of a large family that is made up of every tribe, tongue, and language. By grace, God has granted you the wisdom to understand His gospel and the mystery of the Church, which is the bringing together of all nations in Christ. Therefore, you have brothers and sisters all over the world. Make no mistake about it: God does not see you as unintelligent. To the contrary, He sees you as wise. Wise because you trusted in Jesus Christ for your salvation and this by the grace of God.

In Him we have obtained an inheritance, having been predestined according to the purpose of Him who works all things according to the counsel of His will...
Ephesians 1:11

As a result of being a part of God's universal and local family, the church, you are now a joint heir (v.11). God has not only given you an inheritance "that is imperishable, undefiled, and unfading, kept in heaven for you" (1 Peter 1:4), but He has made you an inheritance for Christ. The Father gives you to the Son as a reward for Christ's sin atoning death upon the cross. Have you ever thought of yourself as a trophy for Christ? Well, that is what you are. In regards to our inheritance, we will never become divine, but we will live forever in the presence of deity as adopted children of God and joint heirs with Jesus Christ. God sees you as an inheritance to Christ and as a joint heir with Christ.

As I type these words, I am staying in a small apartment on the campus of Falls Creek Baptist Encampment in Davis, Oklahoma. Humility and gratitude fill my heart when I meditate upon all that God has done here. Every year at this great camp, thousands of young people have their identities changed as a result of Christ's transforming gospel. In a moment, they are transferred out of the kingdom of darkness and into the kingdom of God's beloved Son. And God says they are wise, joint heirs with Jesus. Not because of any inherit wisdom, but as a result of the wisdom that comes down from above by grace. Beloved, this is also true of you.

In Him you also, when you heard the word of truth,
the gospel of your salvation, and believed in Him, were
sealed with the promised Holy Spirit...
Ephesians 1:13

You will also be excited to learn that you are sealed (v.13). This important verse outlines the way of salvation. The sinner hears the Word of God, which is truth. He or she trusts in Christ and as a result receives the Holy Spirit, which results in being sealed by God in Christ forever. This means that God owns you, loves you and will keep you. The words of the Apostle Paul ring so true: "Who shall separate us from the love of Christ? Shall tribulation, or distress, or persecution, or famine, or nakedness, or danger, or sword... No, in all these things we are more than conquerors through Him who loved us. For I am sure that neither death nor life, nor angels nor rulers, nor things present nor things to come, nor powers, nor height nor depth, nor anything else in all creation, will be able to separate us from the love of God in Christ Jesus" (Romans 8:35-39).

Remember, no one influences your life more than yourself. You are your own greatest influencer. What are you saying to yourself about yourself? What you say to yourself will either promote positive wellbeing or harm it. Determine every day to see yourself as Christ sees you and speak to yourself what Christ speaks.

In Christ you are: blessed (v.3), chosen (v.5), adopted (v.5), redeemed (v.7), forgiven (v.7), wise (v.9), a joint heir (v.11), and sealed (v.13). Therefore, ignore the voice of the enemy, which is full of lies and embrace the Word of God, which is TRUTH. Your new identity in Christ will never change, but you have to be careful not lose sight of it.

I think it would be beneficial for you to read the identity story of one of my friends, Paul. He wrote the following:

> *When we think about our identity, the tendency for most of us is to think of who we are from a relational or professional perspective. For example, we are a husband, wife, mother, father, son, or daughter. We are a doctor, pastor, teacher, businessman, salesman, firefighter, homemaker, etc. Our identity can easily become defined by who we are, what we do, or the earthly status we achieve in this life. Through Blake's teaching in Ephesians, the Lord convicted me of my improper view about who I am in Christ.*

You see, most of my life has been wrapped up in what I can achieve. I have been driven by educational goals, promotions at work, fitness level, financial status, social status, etc. The societal view of my life has been a driving factor in my confidence level, my emotional state, and my overall identity.

The study of Ephesians showed me that these things do not define me at all and that I had been living my life with a false identity. I was so convicted and encouraged by the Holy Spirit through the passage found in Ephesians 1:3-14.

In order to really understand the depth and truth of this passage, I think you must focus and contemplate on what it says about us. When I really stopped and analyzed each verse and discovered all the adjectives Paul uses to describe us, it instantly changed my understanding of who I am and where I find my identity. Here are some the descriptive words used to define who I am because of Christ: blessed, chosen, holy, blameless, predestined, adopted, redeemed, forgiven, and sealed.

This realization led me to repentance for my selfish and prideful lifestyle. At the same time, this understanding set me free and put me on a path of living a life of victory through the redemption, hope, and victory that I have in my true identity, which is in Jesus Christ.

When Paul grasped the reality of his vertical identity it led him to repentance. This truly is the proper response.

To determine your identity in anything else or anyone else other than Christ is pride at its highest level.

• CHAPTER 3 •

The Truth About You

And you were dead in the trespasses and sins in which you once walked, following the course of this world, following the prince of the power of the air, the spirit that is now at work in the sons of disobedience—among whom we all once lived in the passions of our flesh, carrying out the desires of the body and the mind, and were by nature children of wrath, like the rest of mankind. But God, being rich in mercy, because of the great love with which He loved us, even when we were dead in our trespasses, made us alive together with Christ—by grace you have been saved—and raised us up with Him and seated us with Him in the heavenly places in Christ Jesus, so that in the coming ages He might show the immeasurable riches of His grace in kindness toward us in Christ Jesus. For by grace you have been saved through faith. And this is not your own doing; it is the gift of God, not a result of works, so that no one may boast. For we are His workmanship, created in Christ Jesus for good works, which God prepared beforehand, that we should walk in them.

Ephesians 2:1-10

In Christ, we are blessed, chosen, adopted, forgiven, redeemed, we have an inheritance, and we have been sealed by the Holy Spirit of God. We are loved. There may be things going on in your life that are threatening to overwhelm you. You may feel small and powerless, and your faith is dim. Your hold on your identity is weak and it seems to be slipping away. "Did God really say..." is one of the favorite questions of the enemy. Perhaps because of this, you find your emotions swinging from side to side, wobbling off center and teetering on the edge. In this section, I pray that you will be further reminded of your identity in Christ. I pray that you will find balance and stability, and I pray for the joy of the Lord to be restored to your life. I also pray that you will hear the message of this book.

Tim Keller shares a story about being a billionaire, so if you would, imagine that you are one. You have all the money that you could possibly have. You are fantastically, enormously wealthy and you are taking a cab. In your billfold, you have three ten-dollar bills. The cab fare is eight dollars, so you give the cab driver a ten and let him keep the change. Later, you are thumbing through your billfold, and you realize that you have only got one ten-dollar bill left. You conclude either you gave the cab driver two tens, or you lost or dropped the missing bill along the way. You, the billionaire, have now lost ten dollars. Whatever will you do? Are you going to call the police says over and over again that people are basically good and if one can just believe then anything desired can be done, including going to heaven. It is the New Age philosophy of just looking inside. This is YOUR best life. The world will look you in the eye and tell you are not a bad person and that the source of your joy and peace and the end destination of your pursuit of happiness is found within you by fulfilling your wants and desires and doing whatever feels good. The Scripture says the only thing you will find inside of yourself is death. Apart from Christ, you were not a good person. Apart from Christ, you were not OK. There was and is no better life for you without Jesus Christ. Apart from Christ, you are not just sick and needing to find yourself to get better. You are dead. Dead.

The human race is not essentially morally good. Nor is the human race neutral. The human race is dead, cut off from God, under God's wrath, and unable to do anything themselves to earn salvation. Why? For the same reason that little dog can't get up and come to my wife if it gets run over by a car. It is dead. The dead cannot do anything. They cannot earn their salvation. They cannot draw near to God. Before salvation, not only are the lost dead, they are controlled and compelled by the philosophies of this world and can only claim Satan as father. Because of that, the influences of the world and the philosophy and the

to launch an investigation into the disappearance of your ten dollars? Are you going to direct them to question the cab driver and possibly reclaim your money? No. Let's be honest; you are going to shrug it off. You are a billionaire. What is ten dollars to you?

Sometimes we are overwhelmed. Sometimes we are criticized fairly or unfairly. Sometimes we buy things and they break, sometimes we break things we have. Sometimes valuable things turn out to be junk. You may be depressed or have your emotions swerving here and there. If you are a Christian and you are experiencing these things, it is because you have lost sight of your identity. When you allow this to happen, you are like a billionaire fretting over a ten-dollar bill. You have all you need in Christ. Stop making mountains out of molehills.

Fretting and worrying about things that are probably never even going to happen or sometimes making a big deal out of something that is really no problem at all will place a veil over your spiritual eyes, which casts a shadow over your vertical identity. I know we can go through trials and tragedies. Loved ones and we ourselves are diagnosed with illnesses. We lose people to sickness. I do not want to play those things down at all. They are serious life events, and there is no denying the heartache that comes along with them. Even in the midst of these things, though, let me remind you and encourage you that your identity in Christ is secure. Remember your vertical identity in Christ as you grieve, but grieve not as those who have no hope. When I remember my identity even in grief there is hope.

As a Christian, you are a spiritual billionaire. You have all the spiritual riches that you need. Do not allow the things of this world to overwhelm you, depress you, or cause you to be anxious. Be reminded that if you have Christ, you have everything. It does not matter what material things you lose, what other people say about you, or whatever type of criticism you may incur. What matters is how the Lord sees you. If you are saved, and not everyone is, the Lord sees you as chosen, blessed, adopted, redeemed, forgiven, sealed with the Holy Spirit, and loved by God as His adopted and beloved child. You have every spiritual blessing there is. So, be lifted up this morning and let your downcast spirit be renewed by the joy of the Lord.

The Truth about You

Understanding your spiritual biography will go a long way in cementing these truths in your heart, at least, I know it has for me.

And you were dead in the trespasses and sins.
Ephesians 2:1-10

The very first thing we encounter in this passage is that Paul talks about our previous state before Christ. Apart

from Christ, you were spiritually dead. As you thi about your past identity, previously before coming know Jesus Christ, you were a corpse. That is pretty clea is not it? There is much debate about that word "dead. However, dead is dead. If my wife's little schnauzer wa sadly run over by a car died, when my wife walks out, calls him and says, "Come on, it's time to come inside," what is that dog going to do? Is it going to get up?

Of course it is not going to get up. The dog is dead.

What that means from a practical standpoint for you is that before Christ, you are alienated and separated from God. We are unable to come to Him apart from the drawing of the Holy Spirit. You were unable to come to Him apart from regeneration (new birth). You were unable to do anything to please God apart from Christ because before Him you were DEAD. Cut off. There was no spiritual life in you. You were dead because of the sinful nature you inherited from Adam and Eve after the fall in the Garden of Eden. Remember what God told Adam: "Listen, the day that you eat of that tree you will surely die." He meant a real physical and spiritual death. Because of the sinful nature you and I inherited from Adam, we are spiritually dead.

This is the complete opposite of what the world wants us to believe. The world wants us to believe that there is still enough good left in any person to make it to heaven, you just have to be good enough and do good enough. It

values of this age, which are entirely contrary to God, have a high value. Before Christ, that is.

If you are a Christian, think about how your mind and your life have been changed since you have been saved. How your outlook on life is different. Perhaps even how your attitude has changed, even concerning some of the social ills of our day. Now you see marriage as between one man and one woman, and you see all life as coming from God and should be protected. I am not saying that everyone who believes this way is a Christian. If you are saved, though, your values and your morals have changed. If you are genuinely saved, you should no longer be influenced by the philosophies and values of this world. Now you are influenced by the Spirit of God in you working through the Word of God.

We too all previously lived among them
in our fleshly desires.
Ephesians 2:3

Before salvation, you were dead and disobedient. You had adopted the attitudes and the habits and the lifestyles of this world, but now there has been a change if you are saved. You were driven by lust and compelled by fleshly desires. You longed for sin and loved sin. So not only were you dead and disobedient, you were depraved before Christ saved you. It does not mean you were as sinful as you could be, but it does mean that every aspect of who you were had been contaminated by sin. All the faculties apart from Christ—mind, tongue, eyes, ears, everything—was depraved and bent towards rebellion and all bent towards seeking pleasure and fulfilling the desires of lust and a corrupt heart.

Before Christ saved you, you were by nature under wrath. It is vitally important for you to understand that if you are not saved, this is where you still are. Your location, spiritually, is under the wrath of God. If you are not saved, you are not redeemed. If you are not redeemed, you are not forgiven, and you are not blessed. You are not sealed. On the contrary, if you are not saved, you are dead, disobedient, depraved, and doomed to Hell.

How Do I Become a Christian?

I remember talking to a man prior to writing this book and he said, "Yeah, but I am not that bad." No one thinks they are that bad. By that bad they mean bad enough to go to Hell. That is part of the lie of our sinful nature. Romans 1:18-20 echoes the sentiment here but it adds at the end, "They are without excuse." God has made Himself known. It does not matter how good you think you are. You may think you are a morally good person, but if you have never surrendered your life to Christ, you are spiritually dead. Moreover, any good thing you try to do to prove you are not that bad is nothing more than a filthy rag to God. It is motivated by pride. It is motivated by a desire to be your best self, save yourself and do it your own way. You have to come to a place in your life where you realize that is not possible, though. Salvation is about admitting that we cannot do it. "Nothing in my hand I bring, simply to the cross I cling," says the old hymn. It is saying to the Lord, "I have nothing good to offer you. I need everything from you." You and I need everything from God, and He needs nothing from us. This is surely what Jesus meant when He said, "Blessed are the poor in spirit for they shall inherit the kingdom of God" (Matthew 5:3). It is that spiritual poverty that we must bring to Christ.

You see, God is holy. He is holy, and as much as we would like God to lift the edge of the rug and sweep all our sin underneath it, He is not going to do it. A person might do that. A sinful human might say, well no harm done and lift the corner of the rug, but the dirt would always be there. The rug covering it would never be big enough to cover all the sin that would have to go under it. God is too righteous and holy to let that stand. God's righteous character, His holy nature, and His justice all demand that sin be dealt with. God is holy, sin is wickedness, and He must respond with wrath.

But here is the good news: You do not have to experience God's wrath. Christ is our propitiation. That means Jesus Christ and His death on the cross satisfied the wrath of God on your behalf and on behalf of the whole human race. He who knew no sin became sin. Jesus died as your sin substitute. Jesus went to the cross, took your sin upon Himself and there upon the cross He absorbed the full cup of God's wrath against the sin and wickedness of humanity. God poured out His wrath on sin when Christ died for you. The cup is empty. "It is finished," Jesus said. You are no longer required to experience the wrath of God against your sinful nature. You just simply need to repent of your sin and come to Jesus in faith. If you will surrender your life to Jesus as your Lord and Savior, you will be saved. Your identity will be changed. You will be transferred from the kingdom of darkness into the kingdom of God's beloved Son. You will be redeemed, chosen, forgiven, sealed and loved. You will be made holy.

But every day that you live your life for yourself without being saved, without surrendering your life to Jesus Christ, you live a life of deadness, depravity, disobedience, and doom. But if you are a Christian, this is not who you are any longer. Praise the Lord!

Your Christian Biography

Listen, dear Christian, who were you? What is your Christian biography? It is not, "I went to this school, had these parents, went to these camps, played these sports, went to work here or graduated from this college, got married to this person and had this or that job." That is your natural biography. Your Christian biography is different. You were dead in your sin, "but God who is rich in mercy and because of His great love which He had for us made us alive in Him in Christ." Even though you were dead in sin, you have been saved by grace and made alive in Christ. Hallelujah!

Together with Christ Jesus, He raised you up and seated you in the heavens. Here is your Christian biography. Apart from Christ you were dead in sin. Because of God's grace, you are now united with Christ and spiritually alive. You are no longer a dead dog on the wide road that leads to destruction. You can jump and run to your Master when He calls. That is what it means to be saved. You have been made alive while you were once dead in your sin and trespasses.

But God, being rich in mercy,
because of the great love with which He loved us.
Ephesians 2:4

However, the emphasis is not placed upon you as if you did something to deserve this salvation. The emphasis is upon God's character. He is a merciful God. Holy, just, and full of wrath against sin, yes, but also *merciful* and He has a *great love.*

Even when we were dead in our trespasses, made us alive
together with Christ-- by grace you have been saved.
Ephesians 2:5

If you are saved, how could you not have joy when you are reminded of these truths? In v.5, it says God "made us alive together with Christ." The verb "made," in the original Greek, governs the whole phrase. God *made* you alive. Just as Jesus called Lazarus from the tomb, so He called you. Mary and Martha's brother, Lazarus, was dead. Jesus arrived at the tomb and Lazarus had already been in the grave for four days. His decomposing body would surely have an odor that would continue to get worse. In spite of the fact that Lazarus was dead, smelled dead, and was already in the tomb, Jesus bid them to roll away the stone. When they did, He cried out, "LAZARUS. COME FORTH." When Jesus Christ called the dead corpse by name, it received life and came walking out. Jesus Christ made Lazarus, who was once dead, alive.

On April 14, 2000, Blake Gideon, who had been dead, disobedient, depraved, doomed, apart from Christ, spiritually dead, and smelling like spiritual death, at about two o'clock in the afternoon was called by name by Jesus Christ. "Blake Gideon, COME FORTH" (metaphorically speaking) and Blake was brought from spiritual death to life with Christ.

When was it for you? Can you recall? You may not know the exact day, time, or month, but you know around when it happened. If you are not sure or if you say, "I think I was saved," that is really dangerous for you. Most people would say they would never play Russian roulette, but that is exactly what you are doing if you are unsure of your salvation. On the other hand, beloved, if you are certain of your salvation, then rejoice in the reality of your new identity.

He raised us up with Him and seated us with Him in the heavenly places in Christ Jesus.
Ephesians 2:6

The Life Synergistic

The Greek word in this verse for "raised up" is the root of the English word *synergy*. It is a compound word made from sync. Most people have synced a phone or synced their watch with someone else's. Notice this, He raised you up with Christ, which means you are no longer dead. Spiritually, you are now synced with Jesus. Now you have life, but he says in v.6, you have been raised up with Christ, saved by grace "together with Christ Jesus He also raised us up and seated us in the heavens." *Seated* is past tense. It is something that has already happened.

This refers specifically to two things. You have a place of authority and you have a place of superiority. You will never be divine or be God, but you hold a place of superiority and authority over sin. He has seated you in the place of superiority. You have been seated in the place of authority. You have power over sin and the devil. He has seated you in the heavens. This is one of those instances in the Bible that has a "now but not yet" aspect.

It means God already sees you now as you will be one day. One day, the Lord is coming. One day you are going to receive a glorified body. One day you will physically reign with Christ—one day soon, in fact, and that is true for everyone who has been born again. The Lord, who is transcendent, outside space and time, already sees you as you will be one day. He already sees you seated and reigning with Him. Therefore, the Scripture refers to it in the past tense. Not only do you currently have superiority and authority over sin and darkness, but God speaks of it as something that has already been accomplished. In His infinite foreknowledge, He already sees you as you will be one day. Your salvation in Christ is eternally secure.

So that in the coming ages He might show the immeasurable riches of His grace in kindness toward us in Christ Jesus.
Ephesians 2:7

Lastly, notice what he says in Ephesians 2:7. "So that in the coming ages He might display the immeasurable riches of His grace through His kindness to us in Christ Jesus..." This means that God will display His grace through you forever. That is how secure your salvation is. God saved you in order to display His grace through you forever. Not only are you a spiritual billionaire, recipient of every spiritual blessing in the heavenly places and seated in the heavenlies, you are also an instrument of God's reflective glory. He saved you in order to put His glory on display.

Salvation is a gift. It is the gift of God's grace to whosoever will accept it. It is not produced by anything we can do, but it produces in us, when it is genuine, a desire to do good things for the Kingdom of God. Just like peace, love, joy, patience, kindness, etc., are the fruit of the spirit living within the believer, good works are the fruit of that salvation. Good works should be a natural result of salvation. Works, in other words, are not the root of our salvation but they are the fruit of it. Salvation is not just a renewed morality or a commitment to make yourself the best you can. "If anyone is in Christ, he is a new creation... (2 Corinthians 5:17)."

For we are His workmanship, created in Christ Jesus
for good works, which God prepared beforehand,
that we should walk in them.
Ephesians 2:8

"For we are His creation." It is the doctrine of regeneration, the new birth. You may have the same body, but you are not the same person. You have been born again. You have been made new, not reformed. You didn't just grow wiser and become more mature. You experienced a radical new birth. The Reformers said, "It is faith alone that justifies but faith that justifies can never be alone." You are saved by faith that produces good works. Good works are the fruit of your salvation.

God's Workmanship

"For we are His creation created in Christ Jesus for good works." Some of your Bibles will say we are His workmanship. That word in the Greek is *poema*. Scholars believe that this is where we derive our word "poem." You are God's work of art and He is still at work on you.

In 1855, the American poet Walt Whitman published his classic work of American literature and poetry, *Leaves of Grass*. Although it is doubtful that Whitman was a Christian, judging from the content of his work, he was a dedicated craftsman. He lovingly rewrote and edited each poem in the book throughout his life, so there are several editions of the same book ending with the one he was working on at the time of his death. He was not finished, but I want you to know, God is not the kind of poet to let even death stop Him from finishing His work. We know this to be true because when our lives are spent, He will call us home and we will finally be glorified into our final edition. Though the Spirit who is at work in us, editing and reshaping us, God already has the perfect final edition in mind. When we look like Jesus from cover to cover, He will be proud to display us to His glory as a work of art, a poem of His grace.

This poem was written by Chris Tomlin, who adapted an original hymn by John Newton:

Amazing grace how sweet the sound
That saved a wretch like me
I once was lost, but now I'm found
Was blind, but now I see

'Twas grace that taught my heart to fear
And grace my fears relieved
How precious did that grace appear
The hour I first believed

My chains are gone I've been set free
My God, my Savior has ransomed me
And like a flood His mercy reigns
Unending love, amazing grace

The Lord has promised good to me
His Word my hope secures
He will my shield and portion be
As long as life endures

The earth shall soon dissolve like snow
The sun forbear to shine
But God, Who called me here below,
Will be forever mine.

Following, is the identity story of Lon. This is his story as it relates to identity and workmanship:

> *"Are you doing your part?" In many respects, that is a vague question. I mean, tell me what my part is and I'll tell you if I am doing it, right? But when asked within the context of Ephesians 4:1-6, the question becomes much clearer. Then it sounds more like, "Are you doing your part to promote and foster unity within the local church, and, more specifically, within the overall*

Church, which is the Body of Christ?" Well, in order to answer that, I still need to understand what, exactly, is my part.

It would be easy for one to think the answer to that question is found in what I do as a member of the body. Meaning, am I involved in enough church activities to be able to say I am doing my part? If the measure of my effectiveness as a Christian is measured by the extent to which I serve, or by the level of church activities with which I am involved, then I could make the argument that I am doing my part. I serve as a deacon. I teach a connection group. I serve on committees. I have helped lead and administrate a leadership development program in the church. I am involved. But does serving in all those capacities truly mean that I am doing my part? Some would argue yes. The danger in that is that it is completely possible for someone to be serving (read, "doing") so much, that they begin to equate their serving (doing) with having a personal relationship with Christ or even determine their identity by what they do or don't do. Honestly, this has happened to me...more than once. Recently. That is not easy to admit, but it is easy to let happen.

It never begins that way. In fact, hopefully, the reason why anyone decides to serve in the church in any capacity is because of their love for Jesus and their belief that He wants them to serve in that particular capacity. But over time, as you decide to take on more, the enemy deceives you into believing that you have got so much to do, that you better get up early tomorrow, skip the time you normally spend with the Lord, and get started early. It is okay, you are busy, and you have a lot to do. Except one day turns to two, and then two days turn into a week. But you are serving, so it is okay. Then you are asked to serve in another capacity. Sure, you would be happy to serve on that committee, or go on that trip, or teach that class. After all, you are serving! Eventually, you end up substituting your time with the Lord for your Sunday school lesson prep time because, hey, you are still in the Word, right? After all, you are serving! Except that now you are spending your Saturdays preparing lessons when you should be spending time with your family! You haven't spent any real time with the Lord in what seems like months. What does that lead to? For me, it leads to not spending time in prayer except with my kids at bedtime and dinner time; yelling at my kids for, well, being kids; neglecting quality time with my wife; neglecting household responsibilities; trying to do too much and accomplishing too little; and trying to pretend that everything is okay, that I am still a "good" Christian, and that I have it all together. That is not exactly promoting unity in the home, in the church or anywhere else for that matter. That certainly does not depict unity with Christ!

So if "doing stuff" does not mean I am doing my part, what does? At the risk of making it too simple, the answer is found in verses 1 and 2 of Ephesians Chapter 4: "...to walk in a manner worthy of the calling to which you have been called, with all humility and gentleness, with patience, bearing with one another in love, eager to maintain the unity of the Spirit in the bond of peace." What does that mean, exactly? Well, if I am a Christian, I have been called to follow Christ. That means I am to do my best to be like Him. The easiest way to become more like someone is to spend time with him or her, of course. In order to be more like Christ, I have to spend time with Him...a lot of time with Him! That means daily! I need to read and study the Word of God. I need to spend time in prayer, having serious two-way conversations with God (talking and listening!). What I find is this: As I spend more time seeking Jesus and spending time with Him, I become more like Him without having to work so hard to do it. The less time I spend with Him, the less I become like Him even though I have to work harder to do it. It is an incredible paradox. The more I am away from Christ, the more prideful I am and the harder I have to practice humility. But the more I am with Christ, the more humble I become and the less I have to work on my pride. Not that I ever truly stop working on being less prideful, but you get the point. The more I am with Christ, the better father I become, the more meaningful time I spend with my wife, and the more patient I am with just about everyone. More directly, the more I am with Christ, the humbler I become, the gentler I become, and the more patient I become, bearing with one another in love. That is the work of the Holy Spirit in me, and that is what draws others to Christ. It is only when that happens that I am truly "doing my part" to promote unity within the church. So what does it mean to do my part? It is seeking to spend time with my Savior, so that I can become more like Him, so that He can continue to do His part...in me.

• CHAPTER 4 •

Are You Doing Your Part?

I therefore, a prisoner for the Lord, urge you to walk in a manner worthy of the calling to which you have been called, with all humility and gentleness, with patience, bearing with one another in love, eager to maintain the unity of the Spirit in the bond of peace.
There is one body and one Spirit--just as you were called to the one hope that belongs to your call--one Lord, one faith, one baptism, one God and Father of all, who is over all and through all and in all.
Ephesians 4:1-6

When I played football in high school, our team was not that good. I am not even going to try to sugar coat it. We did win a few games, but our problem was that we were just not that big. Our offensive line was pretty small for rural Oklahoma. At that time, I weighed 200 pounds and played on the offensive line. I remember one game in particular where we were terribly oversized by the opposing team. Their defensive line was massive. Massive as in, they were double our size. We were doing the best we could to hold them as an offensive line but the truth is, we were just over powered. More often than not it was their team opening up holes in our line and not the other way around. As a result, our running back was not having a very good game. He was gaining a few yards, but not getting very far. He became very frustrated and started to scream and yell at the offensive line, "You guys are not working, you guys are not doing you part," and so on.

This went on for several plays, and finally, the rest of us had all had enough. We knew we were working hard and pushing back. They were just bigger and stronger than us. So, we decided to teach him a lesson. We conspired together and decided that on the next play, we were just not going to block at all. We got down, they started the play, and we let the defense run right through us. They mauled the entire backfield for about a five-yard loss.

Of course, the coach was furious, but we earned the respect of the running back. Not only did it shut him up for the rest of the game, he didn't say a word for the rest of the season.

Now, there are two lessons that we can learn from that story. One is that when you do not have unity, you are going to have failure. We also learn another invaluable lesson: You can be united for the wrong purpose. To one extent, we were not unified. The offensive line and the running back were not working together. As a result, there was overall failure. We did have unity in the offensive line because we came together in a unified manner to teach the running back a lesson. Let's be honest though, we were unified for the wrong reason.

If you are not careful, it can be like that in life. Surely, you know by now that if there is no unity in your life, then there is going to be chaos. If there is no unity in your marriage, there is going to be chaos. If there is no unity in your church, there is going to be chaos, but unity is not to be sought at any cost. It is possible to be unified in the wrong things. There are marriages, churches, and organizations that are united, but for the wrong reasons. That can be harmful.

I therefore, a prisoner for the Lord,
urge you to walk in a manner worthy of the calling to
which you have been called.
Ephesians 4:1

I want to discuss being unified for the right reason and being unified with one single goal. That is the thrust of this passage. In Ephesians chapter 4, Paul is talking to the Church about unity. In the first three chapters of the book of Ephesians, Paul has eloquently laid out before us biblical doctrine. Then in chapter 4, verse 1, we have "Therefore." Paul always uses this to point his readers back to what he has just said. In light of that doctrine, therefore, he is saying, this is how you live it out. Chapter 4 gives you the practical application of all that has come before in the book. You have been reminded of who you are in Christ and how that relationship has changed your identity. You are blessed with every spiritual blessing in the heavens. You are chosen in Him. You are adopted into His family. You are redeemed and forgiven by His blood. You are wise and a joint heir with Jesus, and you are sealed by the Holy Spirit of God. You were once dead in sin, but now you are made alive in Christ. Before, your life had no purpose; now you are seeking to walk in the works He has predetermined for you to walk in. Or at least I pray you are.

The Church is now one body because of all these things and because of the unity all Christians have in Christ. You are no longer an enemy of God. You are no longer separated from God. You are no longer dead in sin. Your life is no longer useless. It is worth repeating: you are blessed, chosen, redeemed, forgiven, wise, a joint heir, sealed by the Holy Spirit, raised up with Christ, and you are His workman and His workmanship. How should you respond to such glorious grace? How should you respond to such a glorious truth that is yours not because you earned it but because it is a gift of God's Grace?

In a manner worthy of my calling

The verse goes on to say, "I [Paul] urge you to walk in a manner worthy of the calling to which you have been called." There is a lot of emphasis here on the word "urge." I urge you because of God's love. I urge you and I exhort you with every fiber of my being to walk in a manner that is worthy of your calling because of the love and grace and mercy of God. You see, it is quite different than what God extended to the Jews of the Old Testament. God said to the Jew, "obey me and I will bless you." God is saying to us in this passage of Scripture, "because I have blessed you, obey me."

What does it mean to walk in a manner worthy of your calling? You may think that only the pastor has a calling, but the reality is that every Christian has a calling. You are redeemed. You are to live a redeemed life. You were dead in sin but now you are raised up from the dead. You are called to a life of resurrected power and righteousness. You are a child of the King. Your seat is at the table, not in the dumpster. You are to pursue holiness, not wickedness. It is a calling to holiness, purity, truth and righteousness. To live a life worthy of your calling is to live life in such a way that you bring honor and glory to the name of Jesus Christ. Your motivation to do this is what God has already done for you. You would do well to take time every day to dwell and meditate on all the spiritual, material, and physical benefits you have in

Christ. If you were to do this, your heart would be overjoyed constantly.

"Brothers, I do not consider that I have made it my own.
But one thing I do: forgetting what lies behind
and straining forward to what lies ahead,
I press on toward the goal for the prize
of the upward call of God in Christ Jesus."
Philippians 3:13-14

Unity

A casual look at popular culture today will reveal that the world has a very different concept of unity than the one displayed in the Bible. Movies, series, books, and even Broadway plays show that unity, in the world, means my way or the highway. Ultimatums are delivered with a dramatic flourish. The crisis point revolves around the question: Are you with me or not? Then the true love of one of the characters overcomes the other person's bad habits and terrible fashion sense, and they all live happily ever after.

Forcing someone else into a mold is not unity. Unity is not about making someone else conform to your ideal version of how he or she should act or think. Godly unity is completely different. My wife and I have unity in our marriage. We came from very diverse backgrounds. She was raised much differently than I was and that brought a lot of diversity to our relationship. The world says that if you want unity, then one person has to force the other person to change. This is not biblical nor is it smart or healthy. You see, the goal of unity is to get your diversity working together. Another way to look at marriage is two people whose personal weirdness and unique traits work together, in love, toward a common goal. In order to get your diversity working, you have to have the same goal and the same purpose.

A good picture of this takes place on the ice with a pair of figure skaters working together. Each of them does different things. One person might be dancing one way; the other person might be picking the other person up. The man might have the woman draped artfully over his shoulder. The woman might be sailing through the air in a magnificent leap. They might both fall, or they might both perform perfectly or any combination of these or other things. They are performing their own different part of the same skating routine, but they have a common goal and a common purpose. They want the gold medal. My wife and I are not trying to win a medal. Our treasure is not of this world. Our goal is to love God with all our heart, soul, mind, and strength and to finish this race together. Is not that the greatest commandment? Because we have the same goal, our diversity works together in unity to achieve it.

We do this because Jesus is God's Son. Because Jesus left the glories of heaven, came to the earth clothed in human flesh, and went to the cross to die in the place of sinful humanity. Because Jesus took the sin of all humanity upon Himself, absorbing the wrath of God upon the cross. Because Jesus died for the sins of the world. Because Jesus was buried then rose again three days later.

Because Jesus.

I want to seek to please Him as a son, a husband, a father, a pastor, and a citizen. It is the gospel that motivates me, and I hope it's the same for you. It is because of Jesus Christ, I do what I do. Jesus Christ is my identity. I pray with every fiber of my being that anyone who reads this will have the same burden, and I pray the same for you.

> *I therefore, a prisoner for the Lord, urge you to walk in a manner worthy of the calling to which you have been called, with all humility and gentleness, with patience, bearing with one another in love. (Ephesians 4:1-2)*

Essential Elements of Unity

First of all, you must model the person of the gospel. You must seek to be Christ-like in your life. Christians are exhorted in Ephesians 4:1-2 to an internal attitude of the heart. "Walk in a manner worthy of the calling to which you have been called, with all humility and gentleness, with patience, bearing with one another in love." These are not just motions we go through. This is not an outward mask or convention to which we cling on Sunday morning. You can try to model these things by your own strength, but no one will be fooled for long. The attitude of the heart should be one of humility, gentleness, and patience. One believer should accept another in love, however strange and unlike others they are.

Pastors usually hear, at this point, something like, "Well, that's a lot easier said than done." The pastor would know. The pastor has to handle matters involving church members who do not get along all the time. The pastor deals with the ramifications when one person does not accept the other in love, and one of them leaves or stirs up trouble or causes someone else to leave. Every time I look at the cross, though, I see the humility of Jesus Christ. He allowed the very people whom He created to mock Him and spit upon Him and then eventually to crucify Him. "He was in the world, and the world was made through Him, yet the world did not know Him" (John 1:10). Paul also understood the cross as the greatest display of humility and encouraged us to have the same mind in Philippians 2:5-11. This should be the attitude of every believer. This should be the heart and mind of everyone who calls upon the name of the Lord. This should be your attitude.

One of the great attributes of God that you can exemplify is humility. Selfless love. Putting the well-being and the good of others before yourself. This is not natural, so do not feel bad if it is difficult. The natural thing is for us to be prideful and selfish. We may demand our own way and get our say in any argument or disagreement. The type of humility this passage is talking about is a supernatural work. With Christ, all things are possible.

Keep in mind, we live in a day of self-exaltation. The theme of our culture is Frank Sinatra's song, "I Did It My Way." That song is often heard at funerals and, ironically, will probably be piped in 24/7 in Hell to all of its occupants. The lost person does it their way. The saved person does it God's way. The world says everything all the time is about you and how nice your life looks on social media. "Put yourself first," the world says. Climb the ladder. Step on other people. Drive the nice car. Make the six- or seven-figure salary.

The Bible says to display humility and gentleness. This means that you are not to be mean-spirited. This may shock you, but there are some mean Christians within the church. As a pastor, I have met a few in the past. Have you ever met one? There are some who profess Christ, but do not possess Christ. You say, "Wait a minute now, they are Christians." Are they? They have probably given themselves that title. Maybe they feel entitled to get their way and do what they want in church because they have given a lot of their money and time to the church. Perhaps you see the problem now.

You are not to be mean-spirited. You are to be self-controlled. Moses was one of the greatest leaders in the history of the world, yet was considered to be one of the meekest of men. When God called him, he complained that he was not a speaker. He had been a simple shepherd since he fled Egypt and he was pretty happy about it. Therefore, God sent Aaron along with Moses to do his talking and, probably, as an encouragement. When it came time to being strong, though, Moses stood fast and held strong. That is what gentleness is; strength under control. It is strength under the control of God. So you are to be humble and gentle.

Then there is the one that most of us would like to skip. In fact, I'd like to skip it myself. Patience. A lack of patience is simply a lack of humility. A lack of patience is actually reflective of a lack of love. (1 Corinthians 13 says "Love is patient.") So, if a lack of patience means a lack of humility and love, then when a person is impatient or unloving, their heart is not right. When the waiters can't get your order right, do you get angry or do you respond in love? When you order black coffee but get a latte, do you throw it back on the counter or do you calmly remind them that you asked for something else? Or do you say nothing and decide to try something new? When the cashier is a little slow, do you get impatient? How you treat the people you encounter every day will tell you much about the state of your heart. What comes out of your mouth toward the people who serve you tells much more. I want to encourage you to look to Jesus and His cross. Be reminded every single day of what He did for you on that cross, and you will be motivated toward humility, pushed toward gentleness and patience. You will learn along the way to accept one another in love, which means putting up with others in a loving way.

If you can't do that, let me encourage you to examine yourself and if you need to be saved, then turn to Christ right now. After all, this really is the main issue. If you are a Christian, then you should act like one. A Christian has the Spirit of God living in them. A Christian has a vertical relationship that informs and shapes their horizontal relationships. If you cannot walk in love, humility, and patience, there is a problem, and it may be that you are not truly saved. Maybe you need to pause, reflect, and pray for God to show you if indeed you truly are saved before reading further.

My wife and I do not always agree, but we put up with one another in a loving way. I am not all that fond of her dog, but she loves it, so I tolerate it. I am sure there are things I do that she does not like, but she loves me and puts up with me because the Lord loves me and she loves the Lord. The Lord would have been perfectly just if He had chosen to snuff out the world like a stray spark and start over or forget the whole thing rather than to come and die in our place. That is most likely what you and I would have done in His place. But Jesus chose to love His enemies and bless those who persecuted Him. The gospel demands that we do the same.

...eager to maintain the unity of the Spirit
in the bond of peace.
Ephesians 4:3

Guard the purpose of the gospel

We are further told that we should be "eager to maintain the unity of the Spirit in the bond of peace." The unity that you have is a result of the work of the Spirit. When you do not walk in unity, when you do not maintain it as it says in this verse, you are grieving the Spirit of God. You are quenching the Spirit of God because the origin of whatever unity you have is the Spirit of God. You should be eager to maintain it if at all possible. It should be a joy to you. Count it a privilege to maintain the unity of the church and with individuals. If you argue at all, it should be over who gets to serve the others this time and who gets to give way to the others. You have a responsibility to keep this unity as a result of the gospel. Unity is cultivated in an environment of believers, striving to be filled with the Spirit, constantly on guard against actions, thoughts, or ideas that might disrupt that unity. Again, it is not unity at all costs. We are not to compromise truth. It is unity in Christ. So, eagerly keep the unity of the Spirit.

The only way to do this is with the peace of God. You must have peace with God. Before salvation, you did not have peace with God. As a matter of fact, you and God were at odds with one another. He is righteous and holy without sin, and you were wicked and rebellious. According to the Scripture, you were an enemy of God (me too). This is why the word reconciliation is so beautiful. As a result of the cross, you have been reconciled to God. You have been made right with God. You are now friends with God. As a result of being at peace with God, you have the peace of God that now enables you to be at peace with other believers.

You are just like me; when I am not at peace with God I am not at peace with other people. Conflicts that arise in marriages are mostly the result of this very thing. It is because one or both of the individuals involved are not at peace with God and therefore they are not at peace with one another. I have encountered young people who are not at peace with their parents, siblings, or someone at school. There is always all this chaos around them, bickering and arguing and nasty comments. Why? Because they are not at peace with God.

Theologically speaking, a Christian is always at peace with God positionally because they are in Christ. Practically, if a Christian allows unconfessed sin to remain in their lives without repentance, it hinders their relationship with God. It puts a hindrance between God and the believer and hinders relationships and affects their peace. When you allow sin in your life or neglect the things you know you should be doing, things like prayer, Bible study, Scripture memorization, and spending time with the

Lord fade from view. Instead, our focus shifts to doing things that are sinful. If you do not spend time with God, you are not going to have the peace that God wants you to have. This is not because God has taken His peace away from you, but you have allowed things in your life to rob you of that peace. Make no mistake about it, this is going to affect the way you treat your spouse, your kids, your classmates, your parents, and other people in general, like the slow driver in front of you. Think about it, if you are not right with God and I disagree with you about something, more than likely you will respond in the flesh.

Honestly, this is where some people who are reading this right now are at spiritually. They have lost sight of their vertical identity. Their relationship with God is greatly hindered, resulting in emotional schizophrenia and bad behavior. That might be where you are right now. Blaming everyone else for every perceived insult or wrong. You might blame your wife, your kids, the dog, etc. Blame, blame, blame....

If this is you, what you really need to do is repent. Stop blaming everyone else and realize that you are who you are and you have the attitude problem because you are not right with God. Man up. Woman up. Take responsibility for your actions and get back to where you need to be with the Lord. That is blunt but it is simple, and it is true. There is no need for interpretation here. Repent and get right with the Lord and you will get along with other people. Have a humble heart and a willingness to receive it as it is: the truth. This is most of the Christian life.

There is one body and one Spirit--just as you were called to the one hope that belongs to your call.
Ephesians 4:1-6

Finally, we must remember the principle truths of the gospel.

"There is one body" (Ephesians 4:4). When you are saved by the gospel, you are brought into the Church, and there is one Church. There is one universal Church that stretches around the world. We have different local churches, but there is one universal Church, the very body of Christ and Christ is the head. We are all part of one body: Baptists, Presbyterians, Methodists, Assembly of God, or Non-Denominational, which is, ironically, also a denomination, but at the end of the day, all Christians everywhere are part of one body as a result of the gospel. That is what you need to focus on, the essentials of the gospel. If you have been saved, you were not saved by a different Spirit than I was. The same Spirit that drew me to Jesus is the same Spirit that drew you to Jesus. We have one hope. One day Jesus Christ is going to return, and you and I are going to receive glorified bodies. There is room to have different opinions about when that is going to happen.

We just need to be unified in the fact that Jesus is coming back. I can praise the Lord about that. There is one hope. He is coming back to get you and to glorify His Church. One Lord, not two or three or a pantheon full, but one. There is only one way to salvation, and that is through Jesus Christ. One faith. One baptism. At the moment of your salvation, the Spirit, which water in baptism symbolizes, baptized you into the body of Christ.

This is a need to focus on the fundamental truths of the gospel. If I were preaching this part, and I have, I would ask the congregation to imagine a miracle wherein we were able to call back some of the great old saints of history. Saint Augustine, John Calvin, John Wesley, Whitfield, C.H. Surgeon, D.L. Moody and then we had Billy Graham to come and stand among them. We would have Methodist, Congregationalists, Calvinists, Pre-Tribulation guys, Post-Tribulation guys, A-Millennial guys, Pre-Millennial guys – and all together under the same steeple. They would all stand together in unity because of the gospel of the Lord Jesus Christ. (Also, we'd have quite a revival because this day and age has never seen the likes of the preaching represented in this scenario.) There would be diversity, but one goal: the advancement of the Gospel of the Lord Jesus Christ. This sort of unity is what we need if we are going to see spiritual awakening in our time. It is time for the body of Christ to come together on what really matters. The essential, fundamental truths of the gospel must be held in higher esteem than any other non-essential doctrines.

"Only let your manner of life be worthy of the Gospel of Christ...standing firm in one spirit, with one mind, striving side by side for the faith of the gospel."
Philippians 1:27

Here I would like to share Brian's identity story:

In a world where attitudes change over time, even day to day, it is hard to know what is right. Before I trusted Jesus Christ as my Lord and Savior, I lived with a mixed bag view of right and wrong. My measure of right and wrong was based on many things. Some of it was based on how my parents raised me, some on society's standards. Some of it was based on my own thoughts. My parents' values were not always based on God's Word, and society definitely moves in a direction away from the surety of Scripture. Then there were the values I created on my own, usually based on my feelings. We often follow the plan of "if it feels good, do it." Because of this, I realized that I needed a firm foundation of what is right. I found that solid foundation in my eternal, Heavenly Father. Decisions of what is the right way to live are no longer based on my feelings or society's changing values, but an unchanging God.

Now that I am a Christian, I have been called to a new life—a life lived in obedience to the one true God. An obedience of gratitude for the price paid for me: that, according to the scriptures, Christ died for me, He was buried and He was raised on the third day.

Even now that I am a new creation, I struggle with the old nature. The simplest of things, like spending time daily in God's Word, is a battle with the old nature. I struggle with starting my day, first thing, in prayer and studying God's Word versus a little extra sleep. It is my selfish desire to meet a temporary physical need like more sleep or just being plain lazy at the sacrifice of a meeting with God, my creator, who loves me. So, how do I live a life of integrity? The best way to overcome is to keep my focus on who I am in Christ. When I remind myself how blessed I am, chosen by God, forgiven in Christ, joint heir with Jesus, sealed by the Holy Spirit, loved with an everlasting love, my perspective sees the eternal and the temporary fades away. Because of who I am in Christ.

• CHAPTER 5 •

The Right Way to Live

Therefore be imitators of God, as beloved children. And walk in love, as Christ loved us and gave Himself up for us, a fragrant offering and sacrifice to God.

But sexual immorality and all impurity or covetousness must not even be named among you, as is proper among saints. Let there be no filthiness nor foolish talk nor crude joking, which are out of place, but instead let there be thanksgiving. For you may be sure of this, that everyone who is sexually immoral or impure, or who is covetous (that is, an idolater), has no inheritance in the kingdom of Christ and God. Let no one deceive you with empty words, for because of these things the wrath of God comes upon the sons of disobedience. Therefore do not become partners with them; for at one time you were darkness, but now you are light in the Lord. Walk as children of light (for the fruit of light is found in all that is good and right and true), and try to discern what is pleasing to the Lord. Take no part in the unfruitful works of darkness, but instead expose them. For it is shameful even to speak of the things that they do in secret. But when anything is exposed by the light, it becomes visible,

for anything that becomes visible is light.
Therefore it says,

"Awake, O sleeper,
and arise from the dead,
and Christ will shine on you."

Look carefully then how you walk, not as unwise but as wise, making the best use of the time, because the days are evil. Therefore do not be foolish, but understand what the will of the Lord is. And do not get drunk with wine, for that is debauchery, but be filled with the Spirit, addressing one another in psalms and hymns and spiritual songs, singing and making melody to the Lord with your heart, giving thanks always and for everything to God the Father in the name of our Lord Jesus Christ, submitting to one another out of reverence for Christ.

Wives, submit to your own husbands, as to the Lord. For the husband is the head of the wife even as Christ is the head of the Church, His body, and is Himself its Savior. Now as the Church submits to Christ, so also wives should submit in everything to their husbands.

Husbands, love your wives, as Christ loved the Church and gave Himself up for her, that He might sanctify her, having cleansed her by the washing of water with the word, so that He might present the Church to Himself in splendor, without spot or wrinkle or any such thing, that she might be holy and without blemish. In the same way husbands should love their wives as their own bodies. He who loves his wife loves himself. For no one ever hated his own flesh, but nourishes and cherishes it, just as Christ does the Church, because we are members of His body. "Therefore a man shall leave his father and mother and hold fast to his wife, and the two shall become one flesh." This mystery is profound, and I am saying that it refers to Christ and the Church. However, let each one of you love his wife as himself, and let the wife see that she respects her husband.

Children, obey your parents in the Lord, for this is right. "Honor your father and mother" (this is the first commandment with a promise), "that it may go well with you and that you may live long in the land." Fathers, do not provoke your children to anger, but bring them up in the discipline and instruction of the Lord.

Bondservants, obey your earthly masters with fear and trembling, with a sincere heart, as you would Christ, not by the way of eye-service, as people-pleasers, but as bondservants of Christ, doing the will of God from the heart, rendering service with a good will as to the Lord and not to man, knowing that whatever good anyone does, this he will receive back from the Lord, whether he is a bondservant or is free. Masters, do the same to them, and stop your threatening, knowing that he who is both their Master and yours is in heaven,
and that there is no partiality with Him.
Ephesians 5:1-6:9

Understanding your vertical identity so you can live your life with influential purpose is the main theme of this book. The idea grabs me. I want my life to mean something. I want the life that I live here on earth to be a life of influence. Now, we are all going to influence people in different ways. We all carry some sphere of influence. The question is: How are we influencing people? We are either making a positive or a negative influence. We are either leading people closer or further away from God based upon how we're living our lives. My desire is for you to understand your vertical/biblical identity so that you will live life with influential purpose. My goal is that when people are around you, they see Christ in you and as a result of that they are drawn closer to Christ.

Now as we talk about identity, let's set the stage.

About the time I wrote this, it was Halloween. There were kids in all sorts of costumes. I saw princesses, Ninja Turtles, a zombie doctor, and even Santa Claus. One of my boys dressed up as a crash test dummy, and another one was a bum or a hobo. Their expectations are really high for the future if this is any indication, but here's a fact: That is how they dressed up but that is not their identity. Both of these boys have made professions of faith and followed through in biblical baptism. They have a love for Christ. They are Christ followers. That is their identity. They may have dressed up this way or that way, but that is not who they are. I have my own identity. My identity has been determined vertically by my relationship with Christ, not horizontally according to the world. Vertical identity is determined from God's perspective.

God sees the believer (if you are indeed saved, this includes you), as we have studied, as blessed, chosen, adopted, redeemed, forgiven, wise, a joint heir and sealed by the Holy Spirit. That is your identity as a Christian. There is great power in understanding that.

When I was traveling to New Orleans for my doctoral orals, or exit interview (or persecution, whatever you want to call it), the thought occurred to me as I was traveling that this might go south. What I mean is that there was a real possibility that this wouldn't go well for me. So, there was a little bit of fear going down there not knowing what to expect. Then God reminded me, "Blake, that is not your identity. That is not who you are. It is great that you are doing it and pursuing your education. It is great that you are pursuing this as something God laid on your heart, but you need to remember something. Whatever happens, your identity does not change. You may not have Dr. in front of your name when you finish. It will not matter what they say or what they think or do because you are still blessed, chosen, adopted, redeemed, forgiven, wise, a joint heir, sealed by the Holy Spirit, and loved by God. That will never change."

So it is for every Christian.

Have you been criticized? Have you failed to be faithful in something that you really had your heart set on? Did you lose a game and maybe you feel like a failure? Or maybe when everything is not going your way at work, you fall into this state of depression. These are classic signs that you have determined your identity horizontally. When things go well at work, you are great. When things go well at school, you are great, but you are on an emotional rollercoaster because horizontal identity is always subject to change. Vertical identity never changes. God will never see you different than as His adopted child.

The purpose of this book is to encourage you and help you understand your identity from God's point of view. View yourself from above, from God's perspective. God looks at you through the lenses of Christ. When God sees you, He sees Christ because you are clothed with Christ, and Christ's Spirit lives in you. I pray that you would begin to see yourself vertically and that you would embrace your true identity.

You know that you do not deserve to be redeemed, forgiven, chosen, adopted, etc. These are not things that you earned. There was nothing in you that could possibly position you to earn God's Love. It is unconditional. It is a forgiving love, received by grace. That grace that we have received, the love that we have received, demands a response. Our new identity means that we should live a certain way. Trust me I do not want my sons living as crash test dummies or hobos.

In light of our biblical identity, what does God expect from us?

Therefore be imitators of God, as beloved children.
Ephesians 5:1

Mimic God

In verse 1 of Chapter 5, we find another therefore. This is always an indicator that you are to apply what you have just learned to what you are about to hear. In this instance, Paul is talking about chapter 4, but specifically v.32, "and be kind and compassionate to one another forgiving one another just as God also forgave you in Christ." He is pointing you to God's love. The word imitators here is from the Greek word *mimetos*, the origin of the English word mimic. He is telling you to mimic God. Our lives should mimic the attributes of God.

When my boys were small, I could sit in the living room, and if I would cross my legs, I could look at one of them and they had done the same thing. Or if I were wearing a ball cap or a sweater, they would find the same kind of thing to wear. They were mimicking their father. Kids will always mimic their parents' behavior good or bad and we need to keep that in mind, but there is nothing bad about our heavenly Father. Therefore, because God is kind and compassionate and has forgiven you in Christ, you should mimic Him and treat other people in the same fashion. Specifically, mimic God's love.

The Father has given to you a pattern you are to imitate or mimic as "dearly loved children." This is important enough that we have to go back to Ephesians 1:5 to get a grasp on it. We've talked about this in **A View from Above**, but here it is again. "He predestined us to adoption through Jesus Christ for Himself according to His favor and will to the praise of His glory and grace that he favored us with Him in the beloved." You are a dearly beloved child because you have been adopted through His Grace. The application of Ephesians 1:5 is Ephesians 5:1. "You have been adopted; therefore, you are a dearly loved child of God." Therefore, because of Ephesians 1:5, you should live out Ephesians 5:1. You are adopted through grace; therefore, you are dearly loved and should respond to that love by walking in love.

What is the greatest expression of God's love towards you? The cross of the Lord Jesus Christ and His death upon it in your place would not be a wrong answer. In fact, I would give an emphatic yes and probably an amen to that one, but let's get more specific. If you are saved, it is because of what Christ accomplished there. The cross primarily accomplished forgiveness. The greatest expression of God's love is that He has forgiven the repentant sinner. So, if you are to walk in love, mimicking God's love, it means that you too should be forgiving.

The greatest expression of love for God in you is when you choose to love others by forgiving them. If you are unwilling to forgive someone, you fail in expressing the love of God. As a matter of fact, if you choose not to forgive, then you have absolutely failed to realize how much God has forgiven you. You see, when you understand how much the Lord has given you, then how could you not choose to forgive someone who has hurt, disappointed, or wronged you? I know that there is a possibility when you read that, your defense automatically went up. Perhaps, there is an argument beginning to form in your mind. Maybe something like this: "Blake, I hear what you are saying, but you haven't gone through what I have gone through. You do not understand." I will acknowledge that some people have gone through greater betrayal, greater disappointment, and greater unfaithfulness to the degree that I have never gone through or ever will. We are not comparing scars here, but I'll give them that. I also know that you're not called to emulate me or any other person you have ever known. No one can fully understand the extent of the suffering through which another has gone.

No one except Jesus, that is.

Jesus was betrayed by His own people. They turned Him over to be beaten and hung on a cross. They had a chance to redeem Him back, but they chose, instead, for a murderer to be released to them. On the cross, in spite of this, He prayed for the forgiveness of the very ones who put Him there, even the soldiers who hammered the spikes through His flesh.

"Well yeah, that was Jesus. You know, He was God, right?"

True enough. So here is another example. Stephen was one of the first deacons of the church, one of the seven. He was a regular human person. Filled with the Spirit, while being stoned to death, he cried out, "Father, forgive them for they know not what they do." He was willing to do this and he was further *able* to do this because he knew how much he had been forgiven. He knew exactly what his identity was and because of that, he had a responsibility to mimic God. Specifically, he had a responsibility to mimic the love of God, which he had received, and to forgive even those who were killing him, and he did so *while* they were killing him.

Be encouraged as you read this. Forgive. Do not forgive because it is easy or because you feel like it. You probably will not feel like it. Do it because of the cross, because of what it accomplished, because of how much you have been forgiven, and because, as a result of the effect of the Cross on your life at salvation, your identity has been changed. In light of your own forgiveness, it is a choice that you must make. This is not forgetting. It may be a day-by-day, moment-by-moment sort of forgiveness. However, often you do it as a reminder of how much you have been forgiven.

Remember, because Christ has paid the penalty for every sin, we have no right to hold any sin against any person, even a non-believer. Instead, mimic God and forgive. Your new identity demands it.

Christ died on the cross so that all sin could be forgiven, and we are not to hold those sins against others that Christ Himself paid for. Therefore, our ability to love through forgiveness depends on our ability to understand our own forgiveness. Robert Faulkner tells the story of witnessing to a destitute group of people in one of our major cities. As he was witnessing to them, he was telling the story about the woman who broke the alabaster vial of perfume on Jesus' feet and washed His feet with her tears and wiped them with her hair. You see, that was a woman who understood just how much she had been forgiven. There she was at the feet of Jesus weeping and wiping His feet with her hair (Luke 7:37).

As he was telling this story, he heard loud sobbing at the back of the crowd. He noticed a young, frail woman whose face was severely disfigured from small pox. He took some time to encourage her and then he listened to her.

"Will He ever come again? I have heard He is coming again. Will it be soon?" she asked.

Faulkner replied, "Yes, He could come at any time."

The young lady continued to sob uncontrollably and said, "But will He wait a little while? You see, my hair is not quite long enough to wipe His feet."

This was a young lady who understood just how much she had been forgiven.

You too can wipe the feet of Christ by exhibiting the humility it takes to forgive. To do this, you must show love mimicking the love of Christ by forgiving others, especially those against whom you may otherwise be justified in holding a grudge. When you understand how much we have been forgiven, you will be motivated to forgive.

He also gave us the love of Christ as a pattern.

Walk in Love

"And walk in love, as Christ loved us and gave Himself up for us, a fragrant offering and sacrifice to God."
Ephesians 5:2

Not only is love forgiving, it is also unconditional. As stated above, you did nothing to deserve Christ going to the cross and dying in your place. God's love was and is uninfluenced and unconditional. As a Christian, you know that you are going to fall, fail, and sin at times but you also know that the love of God has no conditions. It is that very love and forgiveness and its nature that should convict you to pursue holiness. You can see forgiving, unconditional love in the Father. True love is not about giving to get. True love is about giving. Giving in such a way that your only desire is to see that someone else's needs are met. So, in light of who you are in Christ, you should mimic the Father by walking in a forgiving, unconditional love of other people. Because that is how He has loved you.

In our day, love is often perverted. Therefore, some people have a misunderstanding about what love truly is. Anytime God presents truth, Satan is there to counterfeit that truth. What God determines as Holy, Satan wants to pervert. In the next verses, vv. 3-12, we have a list of perverted love.

The world thinks that love is sexual immorality or impurity, lusting after someone or something. The world presents sexual desires in all forms and calls them love. God says that is not love. What that really represents is a perversion of love to satisfy the flesh. Someone who says they love but is motivated by these things is in darkness. In v.6 we are told God's wrath is coming upon those who live this way. It is idolatry, in v.5, because the people who live this way are worshipping themselves instead of honoring God.

If you are convicted of that, repent. Turn to Christ. Ask Him to forgive you and to cleanse you and He will. He will save you, and He will change you today.

Christians are further exhorted, "Do not become their partners." This points to our past identity. In the past, you walked in darkness, but now that you're a Christian, you walk in the light. That is your new identity. You are light. This is not saying that you are the source of the light. Rather, you are like a lamp. You are a vessel for the true light: Jesus. You are in Christ, and He is in you. Jesus is light, and you are in Him, so you too are light. There is no room for boasting here. The only reason you are light is that you are in Christ and He is light. But it is a blessing to know that you are saved for Christ to shine through. This is what it means to live life with influential purpose.

There are two aspects of light in Scripture: The first is the intellectual aspect, that is, walking in truth. Live your life according to the Word of God. Walk in the truth. Promote the truth. Stand for the truth. I have a quote in the front of my Bible to remind me of this. "Grant me to stand with my dying Savior. To be content to be rejected. To be willing to take up unpopular truths. To hold fast despised teaching until death." That is the way that I want to live my life. Content to live in rejection because I was willing to uphold the truth and hold fast to teachings despised by the world until death. That is what it means to walk in the light. Committing to the truth and holding fast to it. There is no fear of being rejected or being unpopular because you know you are called to this life. Know, uphold, and teach the truth. That is what it means to walk in the light.

But it's not easy, is it? You and I are not by nature creatures of the light. That nature is changed at salvation. The light grows and flourishes in the new believer because the Spirit is reflecting Christ through them. That is why it is so important to be in the Word of God. "Let the Word of Christ dwell in you richly (Colossians 3:11)." You cannot walk in the light if you do not know the Word of God and that leads into the moral aspect. Be holy. You are not to walk in sexual immorality, in lust, coarse jokes, or any of those things. You are to walk in holiness. You are to walk in love. You are to walk in forgiveness. You are to uphold the truth. It sounds like a lot but it is possible, and not because you need to try harder. You can walk in light because you are in Christ and He is the Light. You can walk in love and forgiveness because God's love has been poured out into your heart.

He says the fruit of the light results in goodness, righteousness, and truth. These are the three characteristics of a saved person. If someone claims to be a Christian but their life is not characterized by goodness, righteousness, and truth they are mistaken. This is the fruit of the new birth. If you are truly saved, then your life is going to be characterized by goodness, and God determines what goodness is. To be good means you live your life in a way that mimics Him. Jesus did not die on the cross just to take you to heaven. If that were the case, He would have taken you up at the moment of your salvation. He saved you to conform you to His image. Righteousness is when you pursue that which honors God. This is true godly influence. Truth is when you are living according to His Word.

Bottom line, when you live out your identity, you reflect the light of Christ. You were in darkness, but now you are light. Don't fall into the trap of trying to blend the two together. As the old saying goes, "oil and water don't mix." You must actively oppose evil and wickedness. If you say nothing, it is the same as encouraging it or promoting it. You are not to participate in such things either.

Light exposes the things hidden by darkness. That is the nature of it and that is also the responsibility of everyone who walks in the light.

Take no part in the unfruitful works of darkness, but instead expose them. For it is shameful even to speak of the things that they do in secret. But when anything is exposed by the light, it becomes visible, for anything that becomes visible is light. Therefore it says,

"Awake, O sleeper,
and arise from the dead,
and Christ will shine on you."

Look carefully then how you walk, not as unwise but as wise, making the best use of the time, because the days are evil. Therefore do not be foolish, but understand what the will of the Lord is. And do not get drunk with wine, for that is debauchery, but be filled with the Spirit, addressing one another in psalms and hymns and spiritual songs, singing and making melody to the Lord with your heart, giving thanks always and for everything to God the Father in the name of our Lord Jesus Christ, submitting to one another out of reverence for Christ.
Ephesians 5:11-21

Walk in Wisdom

In verses 11-21, there is a call to salvation. If you are in darkness, respond to it. Respond to the gospel. Wake up! You are in darkness. Come to Christ and He will shine His light on you.

Walk in wisdom, not as the unwise. Be careful and pay attention to how you are living your life. Be on alert. Satan has set traps for you all around your life. You need to look at your life and evaluate it to see if there are areas of compromise. Are you neglecting your daily Bible study? Are you neglecting your prayer life? Are you neglecting to attend church? Are you watching things on the computer that you should not? Are you taking second or third glances at websites you should not be taking a first glance at? Are you living beyond your means because you lack contentment? Running up credit card bills keeps you from doing things for the Lord because you are strapped down with debt.

Be alert. These are the things that will entangle you. These are the things that will entrap you. God says you are wise. That is who you are. You are wise, therefore, walk in wisdom. Make sure you are not compromising in certain areas of your life. Make good choices about everything you do based on your study of the Word of God and do, by all means, read and study the Word of God. Continue to read and it will affect your life and all your relationships, and you will begin to walk in power and influential purpose. You will make a positive impact on the lives of those around you for the Kingdom of God. Meditate on the words of this solace poem by Frances R. Havergal:

I gave My life for thee,
My precious blood I shed,
That thou might'st ransomed be,
And quickened from the dead;
I gave, I gave My life for thee,
What hast thou giv'n for Me?

My Father's house of light,
My glory circled throne,
I left for earthly night,
For wanderings sad and lone;
I left, I left it all for thee,
Hast thou left aught for Me?

I suffered much for thee,
More than thy tongue can tell,
Of bitt'rest agony,
To rescue thee from hell;
I've borne, I've borne it all for thee,
What hast thou borne for Me?

And I have brought to thee,
Down from My home above,
Salvation full and free,
My pardon and My love;
I bring, I bring rich gifts to thee,
What hast thou brought to Me?

I think you would agree the words of that poem are very sobering. Now I would like for you to read the identity story of my friend, Craig. It is simply entitled, "The Warrior."

The Roman military was the dominant force of its time, conquering large swaths of the known Western world for several centuries. It is this image of the Roman soldier that the Apostle Paul describes when he talks about the Armor of God in Ephesians chapter 6. Every part of the armor is essential for each Roman soldier to accomplish his mission and to increase his chances of surviving a military engagement. The soldier was trained on its use until he was intimately familiar and practiced in its use.

As a military pilot, I am trained to utilize my weapons system to accomplish the United States military's missions, and I got the opportunity in Operations Iraqi Freedom and Enduring Freedom. I spent a year and a half going through skills training as a pilot before I was allowed to engage in combat. I flew under the tutelage of more senior pilots who showed me the lessons they had already learned. I went through emergency drills, memorized operations limits and studied harder than I have ever had before. I did this not only because it was expected of me, but I knew if I were to be successful in accomplishing my mission and ensuring I was equipped mentally to return alive, I needed to intimately know how to use all of my equipment.

Paul also describes the enemy the Christian is facing. This enemy is a powerful enemy, a "cosmic power" and a "spiritual force." Paul is so serious about how deadly this enemy is, that he twice, in verses 11 and 13, tells his readers to put on or take up "the whole armor of God" so we may be able to stand against and withstand the enemy.

However, as much as I understood my earthly foe and trained with a solid dedication to my craft, I did not take seriously the enemy Paul was warning me about. My commander had issued all armor and weapons to me so that I was properly equipped to serve. However, while I picked up portions of the Armor of God, it was rarely the whole armor and I never trained consistently with a dedication to become an expert in all aspects of its use in a spiritual battle.

So, when the enemy came with his schemes and temptations, I was left inept and clumsy. The enemy easily overpowered me. I was barely able to lift the Sword of the Spirit to strike at my enemy and I didn't understand how to properly use the Shield of Faith to block his flaming darts. The Belt of Truth that held the other parts of my armor together was loosely fashioned around my waist. The Sandals of Peace were unfastened and no longer provided me a concrete footing. The Helmet of Salvation still protected my head from being completely lost to the enemy, yet not due to my efforts to wear it but to the One whose strength fashioned it.

I was an ineffective and bungling warrior for Christ. I fell quickly when facing the onslaught of the world. My identity became wrapped up with what the world told me was important. When I couldn't or didn't live up to the world's standards, the enemy ridiculed and shamed me. Instead of turning to the One who enlisted me into His service, looking to find refuge in Him, I chose instead to embrace pornography, which led over time to a dependence and addiction. As James tells us, that desire gives birth to sin, and when sin is fully grown, it gives birth to death (James 1:14). My addiction led me to embracing infidelity and took me to places the enemy wanted to bury me in. While I was a saved child of God, I was allowing Satan to wreak havoc in my life, and in turn allowing my marriage and family to teeter on the edge of failure.

Yet my Savior is a great and powerful Commander. As such, He allows for discipline of His soldiers when they no longer follow His commands. The attention getting can sometimes be harsh when His gentle words are ignored. He revealed my transgressions against Him, my wife and my family. In this, He bid me to come to Him, confess and repent, sweetly revealing a broken and contrite heart.

The wounds that I had suffered in my battles with the enemy, even though they were due to my own artful use of the equipment provided to me, my Healer bound them up and dressed them. He renewed my strength and began to transform my mind.

He taught me how to put on the Belt of Truth, this time tightly around my waist. No longer would I accept any lies in my life. He securely placed the Helmet of Salvation upon my head, increasing my confidence in the one to whom I belonged. He latched securely the Breastplate of Righteousness, and helped me gouge out Internet porn and cut ties to harmful relationships.

He taught me how to don the Sandals of Peace so that my feet would stand secure on His solid rock. I learned that my reliance on material things or people was nothing more than shifting sand. Only He could bring me lasting joy and peace. He then placed the Sword of the Spirit and the Shield of Faith in my more steady hands, spending time studying His Word, memorizing verses and growing in my understanding.

My Commander and Healer was also my Instructor, Mentor and Coach, correcting me, urging me on, and cheering me. Having freed me from the bondage of addiction, He was training me to go out and seek out men who find themselves engaged with the enemy, wounded, disarmed and unable to fight.

My identity was no longer as military pilot, or whatever Satan and the world was telling me it was this week. Instead, my identity is in Christ, becoming an elite warrior through His power and taking on the **whole** *Armor of God, now more practiced in its use. Through His Grace, I am now a member of the strongest force known to the universe, one that even the gates of Hell will not prevail over.*

• CHAPTER 6 •

Gearing up for Battle

Finally, be strong in the Lord and in the strength of His might. Put on the whole armor of God, that you may be able to **stand** *against the schemes of the devil. For we do not wrestle against flesh and blood, but against the rulers, against the authorities, against the cosmic powers over this present darkness, against the spiritual forces of evil in the heavenly places.*

Therefore take up the whole armor of God, that you may be able to **withstand** *in the evil day, and having done all, to* **stand** *firm.* **Stand** *therefore, having fastened on the belt of truth, and having put on the breastplate of righteousness, and, as shoes for your feet, having put on the readiness given by the gospel of peace. In all circumstances take up the shield of faith, with which you can extinguish all the flaming darts of the evil one; and take the helmet of salvation, and the sword of the Spirit, which is the Word of God, praying at all times in the Spirit, with all prayer and supplication.*

To that end keep alert with all perseverance, making supplication for all the saints, and also for me, that words may be given to me in opening my mouth boldly

to proclaim the mystery of the gospel, for which I am an ambassador in chains, that I may declare it boldly, as I ought to speak.
Ephesians 6:10-20

A recent study conducted by researchers brought out into the open a fact that most of us will probably think is pretty obvious. In their study, they put a clown on a unicycle in an area of a park that received a lot of foot traffic. Clown. Unicycle. A lot of walkers. Researchers observed that most of the people who were not on a cell phone actually noticed the clown on the unicycle. Three out of four in one group did not notice the clown on the unicycle because they were on their cell phones. Others who were occupied like this did not notice the clown either.

You have probably seen people staring at their phones navigating through crowds of people with their peripheral vision. They are prone to run into low-lying objects and sometimes other people. If you have never observed this, go to practically any high school or college campus. I can't imagine being so wrapped up in something that I didn't see a clown riding a unicycle when I was walking, but we often do this with the spiritual world. There are natural things all around us, of course. Sometimes, just like the people in the study who were so attentive to something else, they missed the clown on the unicycle, we are so focused on the natural that we forget all about the supernatural.

Let's make it personal. Any time you enter a discussion about the supernatural or spiritual realm, there are a few things you need to keep in mind. First, there is a devil. Second, you should not be overly fixated on him.

A significant percentage of the world has no sort of faith. They live in unbelief. These people might have some sort of belief set regarding ghosts or spirits, but in general, they think and act as if it is of no significance.

Christians, however, do believe. Along with their belief in God comes an increased awareness of the existence of the supernatural but they do not do anything about it. Christians know Christ. They have confessed Him with their mouths and believe in their hearts that He is alive. They will sing praises on Sunday and hum along with hymns all through the week and readily admit that they will do so some day in heaven with the angels. Yet they live their lives in practical unbelief. Not a lack of saving faith, rather practical unbelief in spiritual matters. Satan is real, yet this group of people live as if he is not. That is not everyone. There are people who know full well there is a devil and they are on the lookout for him. The answers to two questions will determine to which group you belong.

- How much time do you spend in the Word of God on a weekly basis?
- How much time do you spend in prayer on a weekly basis?

Of course, you know which group you are in.

The devil is real. He is cunning. He is deceptive. He is absolutely evil. He wants nothing more than to kill, steal, and destroy you. You cannot fight him in your own strength. For that reason, you should make it a priority to be in the Word of God every day. Not out of legalism, but out of your love for the Lord. Not because you have to, but because you want to do so. You do not want to fall to temptation. Not only do you love God, you know there is a devil. Hopefully, you are going to be in prayer every day because you are a follower of Christ and you want nothing to stand in the way of that, especially Satan.

The second thing is this: Do not get overly fixated on the devil.

The *New Yorker* recently had a cartoon article of a man standing in front of his car, pointing at it, and saying, "I think there is a demon in my bell housing." Some people think there is a demon in everything. They think there's a demon of hair loss, weight gain, and post-nasal drip. Many attribute all bad things to the devil. This kind of thinking is just as harmful as living like there is no spiritual realm at all. Do not live in practical unbelief and do not become overly fixated with the devil. He is in no way sovereign. He is not the Lord. He is not King of Kings. He does not sit upon the throne.

Yes, the devil is real and you need to pay attention, but we do not need to be overly fixated on him. Some ministers build their whole ministries around casting out devils. I am not saying there is no such thing as possession. I am not saying that as believers, there aren't times when we need to pray to have someone delivered from possession, but there is no need to build a whole ministry around casting out devils and rebuking demons. Ministry should be built around the gospel. What you give attention to is what is going to characterize you. If all you do is talk about the devil, guess who is going to shape your conversations? The devil. You are giving him a platform whether you want to or not. If you focus on the gospel, then the gospel will shape your conversations and your very life. You are called to be gospel focused so that all you do and say will be characterized by the gospel.

Satan cannot do anything without God's permission. Remember the story of Job and all the trouble the devil brought into his life? The devil had to ask permission to do any of those things in Job's life. We do not always know why God allows things to happen, good or bad, but we do know God is good and He can be trusted to do the best thing in every situation.

Also, some things are bad in your life because of your own poor choices.

There are present, real life consequences for not doing what God has commanded even if you know you are saved and have eternal security.

Now that you have heard the two warnings, what Paul is telling us here in Ephesians 6:10 is that believers are called to stand firm in the midst of spiritual warfare by God's power with God's armor and consistency in prayer.

Here is another instance of "already but not yet." Already, Jesus has defeated the devil through His death, burial, and resurrection. Already, Jesus has given believers victory over the devil. Ultimately, that is not experienced in its fullness until the future. Even though the battle has ultimately been won, the enemy is very real and he is very powerful. So, even though he has been defeated and the ultimate victory is yours, and you have power over death, hell, and the grave through Christ, you will not experience this in its fullness until you are glorified in the future at the Second Coming of Christ. Yes, you have the victory. The war has been won. It is a promise, but that does not negate the fact that you still have to fight and battle skirmishes against the devil on a daily basis. You have to show up for that fight.

Are you fully in the fight? Are you resisting in the power of God against the schemes of the devil? We have already discussed people and where they stand on spiritual warfare. If you are not in the Word of God and if you are not praying daily, you are not in the fight. You are not only losing the daily battles of the Christian life; you are not even fighting them. You are not standing or resisting. You are a soft target, and as such you will fall prey to the tactics and schemes and the methods of a cunning devil. As a result, your life will be characterized more by defeat than victory. This should not be the story of one who is a child of the King.

It does not have to be this way. If you make a commitment that you are going to get fully in the fight, you will not experience defeat on a daily basis. You will experience victory. No one wants to live in defeat. I'm not talking about fighting for victory. I'm talking about walking in the victory that has already been won and is to characterize your new identity. Don't live in defeat, but live in victory. Read on.

Finally, be strong in the Lord and
in the strength of His might.
Ephesians 6:10-20

The main imperative in this passage is **stand**, v.10: Standing is imperative in a fight. Once you are on your back, you are in trouble. You have to keep your feet. God would not command you to stand against the devil if you were not able to do so. We must stand against the devil with the strength God supplies.

The Bible here gives us three imperatives to stand within the passage and then in v. 10, we have another. Not only is it a command, it is a promise. He says, "I want you to stand, as you are commanded, and you stand the way I am telling you to stand then you will stand. Be fully in the fight. Show up. Put on your armor." It sounds odd in English. Do all you can to stand against the devil, and you will stand.

Standing is offensive. Resisting is defensive. To be fully in the fight, it takes both offense and defense. So you are to stand, and you are to resist, to be fully in the fight, to be both offensive and defensive. There are some who spend their whole lives on the defense. Their Christian life is lived slouched back in a defensive posture. There is a time for resisting, but it does not look like a person taking a nap. You have to have your guard up. You have to be ready to strike a blow or block one. You are not just to be lying there taking a beating.

Therefore take up the whole armor of God,
that you may be able to withstand in the evil day, and
having done all, to stand firm. Stand therefore, having
fastened on the belt of truth, and having put on the
breastplate of righteousness.
Ephesians 6:10-20

You cannot do this in your own power. That is why it says "having done all to stand firm. Stand..." You have to do it in the strength and power of God. It takes humility to admit that you cannot do it on our own. How deceitful and how evil pride is. Pride has destroyed more people than mass murder, terrorist attacks, world wars, and even bacon. Pride. Basically, when He says, "take your stand," God is saying do not give an inch. Plant your feet in the gospel of the Lord Jesus Christ and stand and resist the devil.

Sounds pretty rough. Well, it is a war. It is not a brownie party. It's not a kiddie ride. You haven't been called to afternoon tea or a social event. You are called to war. You have been enlisted in a revolution to rescue the perishing and care for the dying.

Are you fully in the fight? Are you walking in victory or are you slouched over in defeat?

Gear up for battle because of who you are in Christ: blessed, chosen, redeemed, forgiven, adopted, wise, a joint heir and sealed by the Holy Spirit of God. You are loved by God; therefore, gear up, show up for battle, and honor Him, your General, as a good soldier.

The Spiritual Battle

This could be an entire book in itself, but here are a few things you should know.

You are in a spiritual battle.

> *For we do not wrestle against flesh and blood, but against the rulers, against the authorities, against the cosmic powers over this present darkness, against the*

spiritual forces of evil in the heavenly places.
Ephesians 6:12

Your battle is not against flesh and blood. It is not a physical battle. It does not matter how much you can bench press, squat, or how well you are at palates. It does not matter if you are a cage fighter or a nerd fighter. It does not matter if you are a boxer, a martial artist, or a resilient soccer mom. The number of concrete slabs you can break with your face has no bearing on this fight. Our battle is a spiritual battle. It is against rulers and authorities of this world. It is against cosmic powers and the worldly forces of this present darkness. It is against the spiritual forces of evil in the heavenly places. Your war, our war is against evil. It takes place in the heavenlies, not the seen, but the unseen. Not the physical but the spiritual. There is a war raging for your soul, the souls of your children, your family members, your coworkers, classmates, and teammates.

There is a war, and our enemy is wounded and defeated. Think about that for a moment.

We often think that when people see defeat coming, they give up. Our sports culture in America leads us to think that, I believe. The football team that is down by several touchdowns knows there is no way it can score enough points in the remaining time to win, so they put in the second string and let the starters rest up for the next game. They give up.

However, a short study of world history will show us a different facet of human nature. In war, the army that is about to be defeated is often the most dangerous. It wants to take as many of the enemy with it as it can. In 1945, the war in the Pacific was drawing to a close. An offensive was mounted on Okinawa, Japan, as one of the final steps to defeating the Japanese. It would turn out to be one of the bloodiest campaigns of the entire war. After 82 days of intense fighting, the island was taken. Casualties were astronomical; 65,000 American soldiers were wounded or killed. The Japanese suffered at least 85,000 casualties. Over 100,000 civilians, natives of the island, were killed during the campaign. You see, Japan was already defeated. They were fighting a defensive war of attrition to gain time and keep the Americans off of the main islands of Japan as long as possible. They wanted to make the cost as high as possible for the attacking forces, and they were going to take as many with them as they could. They were already a dangerous enemy, but they were at their most dangerous and ferocious in the face of defeat.

Our enemy is facing the same end. He is already defeated, yet he is vicious and determined to take as many with him as he can into the depths of hell.

You may say, "Well I am already saved." Then he will ruin your testimony if he can and take your family, your church, your city, and whatever else he can. The enemy comes to steal, kill, and destroy. If he cannot keep you from being saved, he will do all he can to keep you from helping someone else to be saved.

I know how easy it is to get mad at people. Have you ever wanted to punch someone? Everyone has, even after they have been saved (sometimes, especially after they have been saved). But at the end of the day, your battle is not against flesh and blood, remember? It is against the evil one who likes nothing more than to see the old man or woman rise up. Because when the flesh rises up, it hinders testimony and prevents you from living a life of Christian influence. He seeks to make us ineffective for Christ. Our battle is supernatural. Our enemy is Satan, and the war is real.

The Enemy's Forces

The words *rulers, authorities,* and *powers of darkness* are all military ranks of the demonic army. Just like our military has ranks, Satan's forces have ranks. Some demons are higher ranking than others, but their general is Satan. The Greek word for "devil" is *diabolos*, which means "slanderer." The Hebrew word for "Satan" literally means "adversary."

Two things from the passage: First, in the last part of v.12, our battle is against evil. Paul describes Satan and his minions as evil, but pay close attention to this word found in the last part of v.11, "Put on the full armor of God so you can stand against the schemes..." Not only is he evil and organized, he is very strategic. The word for "strategies" or "tactics" is *methodia*. This is the root of the word "method." The idea is that he has a plan for destroying your life and he is methodically applying it.

Think about this scenario for a moment. Let's say I studied math and only math for a year. I'd be pretty good at it, wouldn't I? Now I want you to think about the devil. Sometimes we think he's this stupid cartoon figure with horns, a pointed tail, and a pitchfork. That is not what he is unless he wants to be. The Bible says he appears as an "angel of light." He is a deceiver, make no mistake, and he has been around since even before God created the world. He has studied mankind for its entire existence. Do you believe he does not know how to trip you up? All he has studied is the destruction of human life. You and all your power are no match for him alone. Neither is anyone else, pastor, teacher or otherwise. However, just one little bit of power in the tip of God's little fingernail, just as an analogy, is more than all of the demons and the devil combined. That is why it is so important to draw our strength from the Lord. You see, this battle is supernatural, but it is also personal.

Satan is not firing missiles from a distance. The word *struggle* means hand-to-hand combat. *Mano y mano*. One on one. The Bible says you do not battle or wrestle with flesh and blood. The battle is not from a distance. The battle is hand-to-hand. The battle is not over there. The battle is upon you. It is not over there; it is right here in our face. That is why he uses the word for hand-to-hand combat. It is up close and personal. That is how it is in the spiritual world. As a matter of fact, remember what Jesus said, "Satan has asked to sift you [Peter] like wheat but I have prayed for you that your faith will not fail." Satan wanted to sift Peter out. Jesus knew this. Satan had picked Peter for special attention. You can be sure that he wants to do the same for you, and you wouldn't be the first.

You have all the resources you need, though. It is a spiritual battle, but God has given all believers the resources needed to win. God has not left us in want. That is where we see the second imperative, "Put on the full armor of God." The first thing that we see in the passage is God's strength. Some translations will say, "Finally be strong in the Lord," and that is an okay translation, but it leaves room for question. The "be strengthened" or "be strong" is what is known as a passive imperative. It is not God necessarily telling you to gird up your loins and do something. He is saying put yourself in a position for me to strengthen you. You have the strength of God. You are indwelt with the Holy Spirit. You have God's power within you; however, you have the responsibility of putting yourself into the proper position to walk in that power and strength on a daily basis. The Lord is saying, "Listen, I have given you my strength so put yourself in a position so I can work through you." Put yourself in a position on a daily basis so you can experience the strength and the power of God, which will enable you to stand and resist.

Just as a real-world example, there is a trend today where people do all their resisting from the couch. What I mean is, there is a whole generation or more of people who feel like they can resist what they consider to be evil reclined with a laptop or a tablet in their lap or a cell phone in their hand. They can resist or protest anything by clicking like or leaving nasty comments on social media. These armchair activists are convinced that they can change the world by clicking through the right posts and saying the right things on them that agree with the other people in their group, but it is a mob mentality that is leading toward the edge of the cliff. Clicks and comments do not change anything. You cannot resist from your couch. There has to be interaction. There has to be actual work. You have to get out into the trenches. This is the way to actually resist, but you can't be sitting; you have to be standing. You have to stand for something, and you have to be physically standing in the right place to use your personal presence and God's strength to do it. Talk is cheap, and it is also easy.

Have you acknowledged your weaknesses? Are you humbling yourself? Do you realize you cannot do it in your own power? You can gird yourself up and you may do well on your own, but it will not be long before you find yourself defeated. Satan knows you better than you know yourself. You have only studied yourself for the length of your life, but Satan has studied humanity for much longer. So it takes humility, but here is the cool thing: When you acknowledge your weakness, it invites power.

> *But He said to me, "My grace is sufficient for you, for my power is made perfect in weakness." Therefore, I will boast all the more gladly of my weaknesses, so that the power of Christ may rest upon me. For the sake of Christ, then, I am content with weaknesses, insults, hardships, persecutions, and calamities. For when I am weak, then I am strong"*
> 2 Corinthians 12:9-10

Paul had what he called "a thorn in his flesh." He had some illness, disability, or something that kept him humble as he went about as a missionary and church planter to, essentially, the entire known world. Just before this passage in 2 Corinthians, he says he prayed three times to have it removed. We have God's answer above. "My power is made perfect in weakness." When we are at our weakest, we are most dependent upon God and His power. This sort of humility, whether self-imposed or imposed by God, leads us closer to Him. You are never so close to God as when you are in a desperate situation, clinging to His Word and praying through every action and decision as if your life depended upon His answer. The truth of the matter is that your spiritual life does depend upon Him answering. The divestment of your strength always enables you to walk in God's power and ultimately in victory. Please acknowledge your own weakness. That acknowledgement is an invitation to God to apply His power to whatever situation you find yourself in.

Stand therefore, having fastened on the belt of truth,
and having put on the breastplate of righteousness.
Ephesians 6:14

Notice also, the whole armor of God in our Ephesians passage. This is the very same armor that Christ has. "Stand therefore with truth like a belt around your waist" (v.14). Soldiers must have a belt. Paul was probably describing the Roman soldier to whom he was chained as he was writing this letter. The Roman with the long flowing tunic would gird up the tail of it with a heavy belt. They would then attach a sword to it. It allowed them the freedom to run and move around, as they would need to do in battle. Gird up your life with truth, it says. Be a person of integrity whose yes means yes and whose no means no. Be a person of truth and integrity. In order to be a person of truth, you need to have the truth in you. Study this Word, the truth of God Almighty. Gird up your life with the Word of God. Jesus did. After forty days of fasting, He was tempted by the devil and everything that came from His mouth was Scripture. Get in the Word and study the

Word. When you do, you put yourself in a position to walk in God's power.

He also says to wear righteousness like a breastplate. A Roman soldier would wear a breastplate of metal or leather to protect the central part of his body and vital organs from cutting, stabbing, or slashing blows from the enemy's weapons. When he says "breastplate of righteousness," he is not talking about imputed righteousness. He is saying not only are you to study God's Word, the belt of truth, but you are also to obey it. If it is the belt, which undergirds your entire life, then it will be a natural consequence that you are living that truth out. If your life is belted with truth, our breastplate will be righteousness because we will be convicted of anything that is not righteous in our lives.

There are a lot of people who study God's Word and know it really well, but they do not live by it. They do not obey it. A soldier studies, puts on the belt of truth, obeys, and puts on the breastplate of righteousness.

The proper footwear for spiritual combat consists of the Gospel of Peace. Not only should you study the gospel and obey the gospel, you should share the gospel. "For I am not ashamed of the gospel, for it is the power of God for salvation to everyone who believes" (Romans 1:16). You will be able to stand if you obey, resist, and share the truth.

In all circumstances take up the shield of faith,
with which you can extinguish all the
flaming darts of the evil one.
Ephesians 6:16

Also, in every situation, take up the shield of faith, so you can extinguish the arrows of temptation. Believe that truth. That is your shield in the heat of battle. When the darts of the enemy are coming in fast, you must have a shield. This is not a tiny shield either; this is a shield as big and heavy as a door to keep the soldier from getting shot full of flaming arrows. It was wood layered with leather and soaked in water so it was as close to fireproof as could be in that day. Do not just go through the motions, but believe God's promise.

The helmet of salvation guards your mind. Meditate on the truth. Fill your mind with it because Satan wants you to doubt your salvation and God's promises and His Word.

Take the helmet of salvation, and the sword of the Spirit,
which is the Word of God.
Ephesians 6:17

Also, take up the sword of the Spirit, the Word of God. Normally, Paul uses the word logos for the Word of God but here he uses the word *rhema*. That is, the spoken word. When you speak the Word of God, it is a sword that draws Satan's blood. You want to draw blood in a war. That is the point: to injure your enemy. There are a large number of Christians who wouldn't think twice about shooting a burglar who turned up in their home but will not cross the street to slash Satan with the Word of God because it requires a lot of work. To use it effectively, you must memorize the Word of God. You have to have a ready answer to his doubts. Jesus knew the Word of God and used it effectively to drive away the enemy.

God says, "I have given you all the resources. Wear truth like a belt. Study. Put righteousness on like a breastplate. Obey. Have your feet shod with the gospel. Share. Take up the shield of faith. Believe. Put on the helmet of salvation. Meditate. Take up the sword of the Spirit. Memorize. Use it. Pray at all times in the Spirit." Part of your spiritual arsenal is prayer. As a matter of fact, this is the most important piece of your armor, but sadly, for many, it is the most neglected.

It does not take a biblical scholar to know that the men and women of the Bible who were most used by God were men and women of prayer. You will also discover that Church history proves the same. I believe it was the revivalist Leonard Ravenhill who wrote, "No man is greater than his prayer life." If you want to be used powerfully by God and stand firm resisting the devil, you must pray, pray, pray, above all pray. You must give yourself to prayer for the rest of your life. Staying focused on your identity and living your life with influential purpose is impossible without prayer. Prayer is how you put yourself in the position to walk in the power of God. Little prayer, little power, but with much prayer, there is much power.

The importance of prayer can be seen in how hard the enemy works to keep you from praying and how easily distracted your flesh becomes while praying. Fervent prayer strikes a punch to the face of Satan. Prayerlessness is an indictment of lack of concern. A lack of concern for the gospel, lack of concern for the lost, and a lack of concern for your spiritual wellbeing and the wellbeing of others.

But if you will commit yourself to be above all a person of prayer, then God will use you effectively. Remember, prayerlessness does not define you; Christ does, so talk with Him daily. I have made this commitment myself. Press forward on your journey with this old hymn as your anthem.

And though this world, with devils filled,
Should threaten to undo us,
We will not fear, for God hath willed
His truth to triumph through us:
The Prince of Darkness grim,
We tremble not for him;
His rage we can endure,
For lo, his doom is sure,
One little word shall fell him.

That word above all earthly powers,
No thanks to them, abideth;
The Spirit and the gifts are ours
Through Him who with us sideth:
Let goods and kindred go,
This mortal life also;
The body they may kill:
God's truth abideth still,
His kingdom is forever.

Now it's time for you to write your own identity story!

For Conferences, Revivals or Speaking Engagements
or more information, contact:

Dr. Blake Gideon
1300 E. 33rd St.
Edmond, OK 73013
405-341-0253

www.FBCedmond.org/pastor

www.PastorBlake.com

Additional copies of this book or other books by
Dr. Gideon may be purchased at your local bookstore
or at most online book sellers, including:

MasterDesign.org

Identityrx.org

Amazon.com

BN.com

Walmart.com